Dr. McKim has served theological education faithfully for more than a few decades and has written more than one book on Calvin. Here he presents eighty-five different Scripture meditations, weaving throughout the Scripture Calvin's insights on the topic as well as his own deep thoughts on the blessings and privileges of prayer. McKim's comments and challenges are those not of a scholar and teacher—even though he is one—but of a humble believer who knows existentially the difficulties, challenges, and blessings of prayer.

This is a very helpful volume that will challenge the reader to think more deeply about prayer, to thank God more earnestly for the privilege of prayer, and most importantly to spur us on to seek his face more diligently!

—**Richard C. Gamble**, Professor of Systematic Theology, Reformed Presbyterian Theological Seminary

A helpful and inviting introduction to a better prayer life under the mentoring of the Genevan Reformer, as conveyed by an attentive student. Unlike the many misfocused guidebooks to the landscape of Calvinism, this accessible and faithful work by Donald McKim actually takes us to the heartland of Calvin, spotlighting his piety and depth—and it does so with pithy yet substantive devotionals. Reading this book could well be viewed as learning to pray from one of the masters, and it thankfully includes some of Calvin's own prayers. How helpful to have Calvin's own words served as such an appealing feast. With many hours of research compressed into each page, this prayer catalyst will be welcomed not only by Calvinophiles but by all who value prayer.

—**David Hall**, Executive Director, Calvin500; Senior Pastor, Midway Presbyterian Church, Powder Springs, Georgia

Donald McKim has collected materials on prayer from John Calvin's commentaries to produce a valuable resource for private and family worship. What makes this guide particularly beneficial is its basis in Scripture. Each entry begins with a biblical passage and includes Calvin's reflections in order to provide instruction about prayer and encouragement to pray. This combination of Scripture and theological reflection displays once again the genius of the Protestant Reformation.

—**D. G. Hart**, Distinguished Associate Professor of History, Hillsdale College

Donald McKim draws on Calvin's prayers to help us with our own. Like the psalms that shaped the Reformer's prayer life, this guide breathes spiritual passion, energy, and wisdom. If, like mine, your prayer life could use a little help, this book will be of immense value to you.

—**Michael S. Horton**, Professor of Systematic Theology and Apologetics, Westminster Seminary California

Calvin's emphasis on the ministry of the Holy Spirit led him to engage with and encourage believers' daily prayers. Donald McKim, with the acumen of a renowned scholar and the care of a nurturing pastor, gathers choice practical texts on prayer from Calvin's writings and integrates them into digestible and uplifting biblical meditations. *Everyday Prayer with John Calvin* affords rich nourishment for your soul and clarifying insights for your theology.

—**Peter A. Lillback**, President, Westminster Theological Seminary

Donald McKim's book *Everyday Prayer with John Calvin* invites the reader to enroll in Calvin's schoolhouse of prayer. This precious little book provides timeless instruction into the nature of prayer and what it means to commune with the living God. Pick up, read, and pray along with one of the spiritual giants of the Christian church!

—**Scott M. Manetsch**, Professor of Church History, Trinity Evangelical Divinity School; Author, *Calvin's Company of Pastors*

Don McKim has a wonderful way of making theology accessible to all. *Everyday Prayer with John Calvin* offers a helpful and thought-provoking guide to better understanding the purpose and practice of prayer in the Christian life, based upon the prayers and reflections of Calvin—one of the greatest theologians of church history. There's no better way to encounter Calvin at his best than in the reverence that he showed for the practice of prayer.

—**Jennifer Powell McNutt**, Franklin S. Dyrness Chair of the School of Biblical and Theological Studies, Wheaton College; Author, *Calvin Meets Voltaire*

Our prayer lives can be—and perhaps often are—tedious and lacking in zeal. While there is no easy cure for this, it is always helpful to have our thoughts guided and focused by others in the communion of saints. In this book, Donald McKim weaves together Scripture, his own theological reflections, and the thoughts of John Calvin to help us focus our minds not simply on prayer itself but on the God to whom we pray. This is a book that will help any Christian who takes the time to read it, to ponder its thoughts, and to adopt its priorities.

—**Carl R. Trueman**, Professor of Biblical and Religious Studies, Grove City College

EVERYDAY PRAYER

with

JOHN CALVIN

EVERYDAY PRAYER SERIES

Everyday Prayer with John Calvin

FORTHCOMING

Everyday Prayer with the Puritans
Everyday Prayer with the Reformers

EVERYDAY PRAYER

with

JOHN CALVIN

D O N A L D K . M c K I M

P U B L I S H I N G
P.O. BOX 817 • PHILLIPSBURG • NEW JERSEY 08865-0817

Printed in the United States of America

Library of Congress Cataloging-in-Publication Data

Names: McKim, Donald K., author.
Title: Everyday prayer with John Calvin / Donald K. McKim.
Description: Phillipsburg, NJ : P&R Publishing, [2019] | Includes
  bibliographical references.
Identifiers: LCCN 2019013789| ISBN 9781629956701 (hardcover) | ISBN
  9781629956718 (epub) | ISBN 9781629956725 (mobi)
Subjects: LCSH: Calvin, Jean, 1509-1564. Institutio Christianae religionis. |
  Prayer--Christianity--Meditations.
Classification: LCC BX9420.I69 M355 2019 | DDC 248.3/2--dc23
LC record available at https://lccn.loc.gov/2019013789

To Westminster College friends:

Bryce Craig
Mike Loudon
Tom McGrath

With appreciation for our friendship,
for good times of learning together,
and for the ministries of each of you

In memory of our beloved Westminster
College philosophy professor,
Dr. Thomas M. Gregory

Contents

PREFACE

F OR some years, I have wanted to write something about the observations of John Calvin (1509–1564) on prayer. I have written and edited other books on Calvin; his theology is deeply rich and has been of key significance to me. So I am especially pleased to introduce, in this book, his insights on this important theological topic.

Prayer is central to the Christian life. In the 1559 edition of Calvin's major theological work, *Institutes of the Christian Religion*, the longest chapter is the chapter on prayer. Calvin had much to say about prayer. His theological views were grounded in his interpretation of Scripture and of the many passages in which prayer is mentioned in the Bible. Calvin built on these interpretive or exegetical findings in order to synthesize his thoughts on prayer, which he presented in the *Institutes* (see 3.20).

My approach in this book is to provide a series of short devotional reflections on quotations from Calvin, which are drawn from the *Institutes* and from his commentaries on Old and New Testament books. My reflections on Calvin explain what he is saying theologically and point out its importance for our Christian faith and lives today.

I have had a vocational passion in the past few years to try to introduce insights from major theologians in an accessible way, through short devotional pieces that each center around a quotation from one of those theologians. In my *Coffee with Calvin: Daily Devotions*, I focused on quotations from Calvin's

Institutes that cover the whole range of Christian faith. In *Conversations with Calvin: Daily Devotions*, I explored quotations from Calvin's commentaries on Christian belief and Christian living. I have also written devotional books on Martin Luther and Dietrich Bonhoeffer using this method.

This book focuses on quotations from Calvin about prayer in its many aspects. As we hear Calvin's comments and reflect on them, my hope is that our theological understanding will be deepened and our lives of faith will be impacted and strengthened through our own prayers.

These devotions, plus fifteen prayers that Calvin prayed at the end of various lectures that he gave on biblical passages, introduce us to Calvin's perspectives—which are based on Scripture—and to what they mean for Christians who pray to God. The devotions here explore different aspects of what prayer meant to Calvin, with some of the themes being reinforced as they emerge through the course of Calvin's interpretation of many biblical passages. Collectively, the pieces open up Calvin's thoughts on prayer, which was so vital and central to his own Christian belief and experience.

I would like to thank the fine folks at P&R Publishing for their interest in and splendid help with this project. David Almack guided me through the early process of the book proposal. Good conversations with Dave and Amanda Martin strengthened the structure of the devotions and introduced the idea of adding Calvin's prayers to the book. To them and their colleagues, including Emily Hoeksema, I am most appreciative.

This book is of special significance to me, because my initial contact was with my friend, Bryce Craig, the president of P&R Publishing. Bryce and I were students together at Westminster College in New Wilmington, Pennsylvania. After all the years, it has been great to be back in touch, and I am most grateful for his support of this project. It is also a privilege to publish with the publishing house that was begun by Bryce's grandfather and served by his father and, so faithfully, by Bryce himself for many years.

This book is dedicated to Bryce and to two of our other Westminster College friends. Mike Loudon and Tom McGrath have both been dedicated Presbyterian pastors with whom I have shared many hours and whom I greatly admire. I am deeply thankful for these three friends and for the happy memories we hold. I honor their ministries of faithful service to Jesus Christ.

The book is also dedicated to the memory of our Westminster College philosophy professor, Dr. Thomas M. Gregory. Bryce, Mike, Tom, and I were all blessed to count Dr. Gregory as our teacher and friend. He was a committed Reformed Christian whose teaching ministry enhanced our lives and our faith. Dr. Gregory was especially kind in helping me to become a student pastor for the three churches of Friendship Parish in Slippery Rock, Pennsylvania. I served the churches during my senior year at Westminster, while I was a student at Pittsburgh Theological Seminary, and during the years of my doctoral studies. I was ordained as their Stated Supply minister, and I am immensely thankful for Dr. Gregory's initiative in helping this relationship to develop. In the further providence of God, my sister, Thelma, met her future husband, Dave, in one of the Parish churches where he was a member.

All my writing is supported and energized by the gift of God that is my family. LindaJo and I have shared married life for over forty years. Her love, through all our times together, is my great blessing, and I thank her from the bottom of my heart for all the support and loving care she has given and continues to give me. Our deep joy is our sons and their families: Stephen and his wife Caroline with our grandchildren Maddie, Annie, and Jack, and Karl and his wife Lauren. They bring us true happiness and are ongoing sources of blessing that we receive most gratefully. We praise God!

My hope is that this book will introduce readers to the

theology of John Calvin as it emerged from his interpretation of Scripture passages on prayer. Calvin's views can enhance and deepen our theological understanding as we live our Christian lives and are part of the church and, daily, people of prayer. To God be the glory!

USING THIS BOOK

THIS book introduces John Calvin's reflections on Christian prayer. I have drawn quotations from Calvin's *Institutes of the Christian Religion* and from his commentaries on the Old and New Testaments. My goal is to provide understanding of Calvin's views and also to suggest ways in which his insights can nourish our Christian faith today. This book can be used for individual devotional reading as well as with groups.

The format of each devotion is the same. A Scripture passage is provided for initial reading. I explain the context and emphases of the passage in the text of the devotion. The order of the devotions in the book follows the biblical or canonical order of these Scripture passages.

Calvin's comments on prayer are provided, and reflections are given on their meaning and importance for contemporary Christians as they pray.

Each devotion ends with either a prayer point or a reflection question. Prayer points suggest ways that readers can incorporate that devotion's insights into their own prayers. Reflection questions suggest further dimensions to what has been described, for reflection or group discussion.

I recommend the following approach:

1. *Read.* Read the Scripture passage at the top of each devotion and then the devotion itself. You can mediate on this Scripture before reading the devotion or can

keep it in mind as you read the devotion. Each devotion is compact, and every sentence is important. Try to contemplate each sentence as you read it.

2. *Meditate.* After reading the devotion, meditate on its instruction, asking questions such as

- What has Calvin conveyed in his comments on prayer here?
- In what ways can the church's life of prayer be deepened by Calvin's insights?
- What do Calvin's observations mean for my life of prayer?
- To what new directions in my prayer does this devotion call me?
- What ongoing changes in my prayer life do Calvin's words point to?

3. *Pray.* Whether or not a specific prayer point appears at the end of the devotion, spend time in prayer reflecting on the Scripture passage, on Calvin's insights, and on the comments in the devotion. Incorporate all that you experience into your "conversation with God" in prayer.

4. *Act.* These insights about prayer may lead you to move into new directions or to act in new ways in your life. Be open to the new dimensions of Christian living to which your prayers move you.

The title of each devotion expresses a main point of the devotion. As you read and reread these titles, recall what the corresponding devotion says.

If you keep a journal, incorporate insights about your encounters with prayer in the journal either daily or at special times in the week. If you keep a prayer list, expand it to include what God's Spirit tells you through your devotional readings. These materials may be reviewed later and appropriated again for your life.

The devotions and the prayers from Calvin can be read either daily or on occasion. Calvin had a robust doctrine of the providence of God and of the work of the Holy Spirit. However and whenever you use these devotions, use them prayerfully and with the anticipation that God can—and will!—speak to you through them.

Two lists of resources are provided at the back of the book: a list of the specific works by Calvin that contain the material that is quoted throughout this book, as well as a list of selected additional resources to enable further study of Calvin's teachings. The first list contains the specific printings of Calvin's works that I consulted for the quotes and prayers that are used throughout the book, but you can find these same quotations in any edition of the same translation of each work (many of them are easily available online).

G RANT, Almighty God, that since thou art pleased kindly
to invite us to thyself, and hast consecrated thy word
for our salvation,—O grant that we may willingly, and from
the heart, obey thee, and become so teachable, that what thou
hast designed for our salvation may not turn to our perdition;
but may that incorruptible seed by which thou dost regenerate
us into a hope of the celestial life so drive its roots into our
hearts, and bring forth fruit, that thy name may be glorified;
and may we be so planted in the courts of thine house, that
we may grow and flourish, and that fruit may appear through
the whole course of our life, until we shall at length enjoy that
blessed life which is laid up for us in heaven, through Christ
our Lord.—Amen.

PRAY AND PROCEED

Genesis 32:9–23

SOMETIMES we pray, ask God for something, and then forget about it. We assume that God will act while we stand by and wait for the answer to our prayer to appear. But this is too simple, and it is not what God desires.

After Jacob had tricked his brother Esau out of his birthright, he fled in order to escape Esau's fury (see Gen. 27). Later, Jacob wanted to be reconciled with Esau (see Gen. 32:5). Before doing so, he prayed to God and confessed his unworthiness (see v. 10) and his fear of his brother (see v. 11). Then he took a present for Esau, and the two brothers met and were reconciled (see Gen. 33).

Calvin saw, in these steps that Jacob took, a prescription for how we should follow through with our own prayers to God. He wrote, "After he has prayed to the Lord, and arranged his plans, he now takes confidence and meets the danger. By which example the faithful are taught, that whenever any danger approaches, this order of proceeding is to be observed; first, to resort directly to the Lord; secondly, to apply to immediate use whatever means of help may offer themselves; and thirdly, as persons prepared for any event, to proceed with intrepidity whithersoever the Lord commands."

First, pray. Then use whatever means of help God gives. Then proceed "with intrepidity," or boldness, to do whatever God commands. We don't pray and then forget it. We pray—and then proceed! We proceed in the direction of our prayer, using the means that God gives and acting to obey God's commands.

Follow through with your prayers: pray; use helps; obey God!

PRAYER POINT: Pray, and ask God to help you to use the helps that he gives and to obey his will.

PRAY TO THE GOD WHO IS TRUE

Numbers 14:13–19

W HEN Israel was in the wilderness and moving toward the Promised Land, the people rebelled against Moses and Aaron (see Num. 14). They thought that they would die, and some of them wanted to go back to Egypt.

But Moses interceded for the people with God. He prayed, "Let the power of the LORD be great in the way that you promised when you spoke, saying . . ." and then recounted God's promise to be "slow to anger, and abounding in steadfast love" (Num. 14:17–18; also see Ex. 34:6–7). Moses appealed to God's word of promise as he sought forgiveness for the people (see Num. 14:19).

Calvin saw in this "a sure directory for prayer." For "nothing can be more sure than [God's] own word, on which if our prayers are based, there is no reason to fear that they will be ineffectual, or that their results should disappoint us, since He who has spoken will prove Himself to be true. And, in fact, this is the reason why He speaks . . . to afford us the grounds for addressing Him, for else we must needs be dumb."

This is our "directory for prayer" as well. We have all confidence in praying to the God who has spoken and will prove to be true to his own self. The God who speaks invites us to speak to him. This is the basis of prayer. When we pray, based on God's Word, our prayers will always bring effects. They will not disappoint. God proves true—ever and always! God is God. We can trust his Word as we pray!

PRAYER POINT: Pray a prayer based on God's words of promise in Scripture.

20

TONGUES BREAK FORTH INTO SPEECH

1 Samuel 1:9–18

W E can pray in two ways: through unspoken thoughts that we direct toward God and through words that we speak audibly. In both cases, we focus our attention on God, knowing that he surely and certainly hears our prayers, whether they are "unuttered or expressed."

Calvin noted that sometimes the best prayers are silent—inaudible to others and known only by the one who is silently praying and by God. He wrote, "Even though the best prayers are sometimes unspoken, it often happens in practice that, when feelings of mind are aroused, unostentatiously the tongue breaks forth into speech, and the other members into gesture. From this obviously arose that uncertain murmur of Hannah's [1 Sam. 1:13], something similar to which all the saints continually experience when they burst forth into broken and fragmentary speech."

The example of Hannah touches us. As she prayed for a son, she was "deeply distressed" and "wept bitterly" (1 Sam. 1:10). Her desire was so deep that she was "praying silently; only her lips moved, but her voice was not heard" (v. 13). Our silent prayers break forth into speech, even when they are not heard by others. Our lips move, even if only in "broken and fragmentary speech," as Calvin says.

God hears all our prayers—whether they are silent, audible, quiet, or loud expressions. This comforts us. It is not the "form" of the prayer that counts but the prayer's focus on God. We can let our tongues "break forth into speech" and know that God hears our words and thoughts—however they are expressed!

PRAYER POINT: Spend time in both silent prayer and audible prayer, focusing on God in both ways of praying.

CONVERSATION WITH GOD

Psalm 4:1–3

PEOPLE think of prayer in many ways. They may see it as something that is uttered in church or as the blessing that is said before a meal. Or they may see it as something that is expressed in the silence of one's own heart. Throughout the Bible, prayer takes place as humans connect with God. The psalmist says, "Answer me when I call, O God of my right! You gave me room when I was in distress. Be gracious to me, and hear my prayer" (Ps. 4:1).

For Calvin, the nature of prayer—no matter its outward form—is that of "conversation with God." Calvin wrote that "for framing prayer duly and properly, let this be the first rule: that we be disposed in mind and heart as befits those who enter conversation with God."

This means that prayer is serious—we are conversing with almighty God. We should not enter into prayer lightly or irreverently. We are in conversation with the great God—the ruler of all! Yet God hears us as we express our prayers. Calvin went on to refer to prayer as "intimate conversation" with God. We can unburden our hearts and minds before the God who is ever-present with us, who cares for us, and whose Holy Spirit guides and enables our prayers.

Prayer is our greatest privilege. Intimate conversation with God is our dearest delight. We thank God for the privilege of communicating with him and of experiencing the wonders of his communication with us—especially through Jesus Christ. Let us pray!

REFLECTION QUESTION: Think about your understanding of prayer. Do you see prayer as conversation—between you and God and between God and you?

PRAYER LIGHTENS CARE

Psalm 10:12–18

S OMETIMES God seems aloof—standing "far off" (Ps. 10:1). Today's psalmist feels that God is hidden in times of trouble. The wicked seem to prosper, preying on the "helpless" (see vv. 8–9) and "think[ing] in their heart, 'God has forgotten . . . he will never see it'" (v. 11). Ultimately the psalmist asks, "Why do the wicked renounce God, and say in their hearts, 'You will not call us to account'?" (v. 13). Yet this brutal honesty the psalmist shows before God leads him to a renewed faith, as he prays, "But you do see! Indeed you note trouble and grief. . . . You will hear the desire of the meek" (vv. 14, 17).

In prayer, we can be completely honest with God—can lament, question, and even challenge God. He is "big enough" to take our barrages! But as Calvin said, "It should always be observed, that the use of praying is, that God may be the witness of all our affections; not that they would otherwise be hidden from him, but when we pour out our hearts before him, our cares are hereby greatly lightened, and our confidence of obtaining our requests increases."

God sees and hears what is deep in our hearts. When we pour out our hearts, our cares can be lightened, and we can have increasing confidence that God hears and answers. We can be honest with God. We can lay out our deepest emotions. We can trust God to hear and strengthen our hearts (see v. 17). We can commend ourselves and all our circumstances—both our hopes and our fears—to the Lord, who will lighten our cares!

PRAYER POINT: Spend time in prayer, letting God know all the things that trouble you—in complete honesty.

Praying God's Promises

Psalm 12

Throughout Scripture, God commands his people to pray. Said Jesus, "Ask, and it will be given you; search, and you will find; knock, and the door will be opened for you" (Matt. 7:7). God wants us to be in conversation with him through prayer and to be people of prayer throughout our lives.

But his commands usually come with promises. The psalmist said, "The promises of the LORD are promises that are pure" (Ps. 12:6)—they can be forever trusted. Jesus commands us to "ask" and promises that "it will be given you." "Search," and he promises that we "will find." When we "knock," Jesus promises that "the door will be opened for you." We grow our relationship with God through prayer as we obey his commands to pray. But his promises that accompany our prayers give us confidence that he hears and answers. As Calvin wrote, "We see that to us nothing is promised to be expected from the Lord, which we are not also bidden to ask of him in prayers."

We can pray God's promises. By faith, we believe his promises that we read in the Scriptures. By prayer, we express that faith in conversation and communion with God. In prayer, we convey our needs, as God calls us to do, and God also meets our needs with the promises that we receive in his Word to us.

It is precious to receive God's command to pray—as well as to receive his promises to answer our prayers. We pray while believing . . . and receiving!

PRAYER POINT: Pray to God, using several of the promises of Scripture. Trust God to hear and answer you.

G RANT, Almighty God, that as thou hast hitherto shewn to us so many favours, since the time thou hast been pleased to adopt us as thy people,—O grant, that we may not forget so great a kindness, nor be led away by the allurements of Satan, nor seek for ourselves inventions, which may at length turn to our ruin; but that we may continue fixed in our obedience to thee, and daily call on thee, and drink of the fullness of thy bounty, and at the same time strive to serve thee from the heart, and to glorify thy name, and thus to prove that we are wholly devoted to thee, according to the great obligations under which thou hast laid us, when it had pleased thee to adopt us in thine only-begotten Son.—Amen.

Commit Your Cause to God

Psalm 17:1–2

P EOPLE give themselves to many causes. These can be diverse: animal rights, human rights, civil rights, poverty, immigration, homelessness—and the list goes on.

People of faith support just causes—causes that are right in the sight of God. The psalmist prayed, "Hear a just cause, O LORD; attend to my cry; give ear to my prayer from lips free of deceit " (Ps. 17:1; see also 9:4). He did not cry to God to cover up his own sins, but he prayed to God with a sincere heart, seeking to be obedient to the Lord.

While people support many causes, not all of them commend their causes and actions to God. Yet this is what Christians do. As Calvin noted, "The faithful not only depend upon the goodness of their cause, they also commit it to God that he may defend and maintain it; and whenever any adversity befalls them, they betake themselves to him for help."

God is concerned with what concerns us. He is concerned with what concerns the world. As Christians, we align ourselves with causes that we understand to be "just" and to express the will of God. In society, these range across many issues. Our commitment to Jesus Christ commits us to doing what we can to live and work for his coming reign. As he instructed us to pray, "Your kingdom come. Your will be done" (Matt. 6:10).

Commit your cause to God. Pray for those causes that are near to God's heart and that seek a just and peaceful society.

PRAYER POINT: Make it a regular practice to include "just causes" in your prayers. Ask God to bless and help those causes that express his will and purposes.

No Calamities Hinder Us from Praying

Psalm 18:1–6

WE can often let "little things" get in the way of our prayers. We get busy or distracted or perhaps think that there isn't anything we "need," and so we omit prayer from our lives.

And then what happens when "big events" occur? If we face great difficulties in our families, churches, or jobs, do we skip our prayers over these things? Perhaps if we've done something wrong, we are ashamed to pray. Or if we are sick, we put our faith purely in medical science. So calamities, too, may hinder our prayers.

When the psalmist faced calamities—when "the cords of death encompassed me; the torrents of perdition assailed me" (Ps. 18:4)—he prayed: "In my distress I called upon the Lord; to my God I cried for help. From his temple he heard my voice, and my cry to him reached his ears" (v. 6). On this verse, Calvin wrote, "It was a very evident proof of uncommon faith in David, when, being almost plunged into the gulf of death, he lifted up his heart to heaven by prayer. Let us therefore learn, that such an example is set before our eyes, that no calamities, however great and oppressive, may hinder us from praying, or create an aversion to it."

No matter what our situation—no matter what calamities come to us—we can pray. In our distress, we can lift our hearts to God. In times when we need help the most, we can pray. Do not let anything hinder your prayers to God for help!

> **Reflection Question:** What have you faced, or what are you currently facing, that you have not prayed about? What can keep you focused on praying to God about all things?

HIDDEN FAULTS

Psalm 19:7–14

W HEN we confess our sins, it is important for us to name them before God as specifically as possible. Doing so will bring to our minds all that we have done against God—the ways we have failed to obey and be faithful. Such confessions show that we have no self-righteousness within us. When we recognize the ways that we have broken God's law and realize that we deserve the consequences of our sins, we know that we cannot justify ourselves. We can only confess our transgressions.

But we will never be able to name all our sins. Many of them we know; many others we don't know. The psalmist knew that God's law was "perfect" (Ps. 19:7). But he also knew that he had broken God's law and was guilty of "errors" (v. 12). Even more, he knew he had sinned in ways that he did not recognize. So he prayed, in that same verse, "Clear me from hidden faults." We have hidden faults too—sins that are hidden to our eyes; sins of inadvertence. Again—no room for self-righteousness.

But Calvin wrote, "God tolerates even our stammering and pardons our ignorance whenever something inadvertently escapes us; as indeed without this mercy there would be no freedom to pray." God does not require us to be "accurate accountants" who keep tallies of all our transgressions. We sin without knowing it or without intending to. But God's mercy prevails!

So we name our sins—the ones that we know. And we pray for God to forgive us for our "hidden faults"—for all that we have done or left undone that we do not recognize or know. We pray, "Let . . . the meditation of my heart be acceptable to you, O LORD" (v. 14).

PRAYER POINT: Confess your sins to God, and ask him to clear you from hidden faults.

FAITH IN GOD'S WORD IN PRAYER

Psalm 22

Have you ever prayed to God, crying by day and receiving no answer and by night but finding no rest (see Ps. 22:2)? This was the cause of the intensity in the psalmist's prayer for today, as he prayed for deliverance from suffering and hostility. He felt forsaken by God: "My God, my God, why have you forsaken me? Why are you so far from helping me, from the words of my groaning?" (v. 1).

The psalmist began his prayer by expressing his deep feelings of forsakenness—he felt that God was not answering his prayer. He continued to remain in sustained prayer throughout the rest of the psalm and sought God's help. Despite his feelings, the psalmist kept on praying.

Calvin noted that in the Psalms, "we can often see that David and other believers, when they are almost worn out with praying and seem to have beaten the air with their prayers as if pouring forth words to a deaf God, still do not cease to pray [Ps. 22:2]. For, unless the faith placed in it is superior to all events, the authority of God's Word does not prevail."

Through our long, agonizing times of prayer, we keep faith in God's Word. We believe God's promises throughout the Scriptures. Our prayers will be heard and answered by God. The Scriptures are authoritative for us; they convey God's unbreakable words of promise.

Prayer is an expression of our faith in God's Word. That Word guides and sustains us, even when our prayers seem unanswered. The Scriptures urge us to pray . . . and to keep on praying!

REFLECTION QUESTION: When has God's Word sustained your prayer life in the midst of difficulties?

GOD GENTLY SUMMONS US TO PRAY

Psalm 25:1–15

ONE of the greatest blessings and joys we have, as the people of God, is God's invitation for us to pray. In fact, throughout the Scriptures, he commands us to pray (for example, in Psalm 50:15), and in the Psalms we find many prayers offered by people who know that God hears and answers prayers. And so the psalmist says, "To you, O LORD, I lift up my soul. O my God, in you I trust" (Ps. 25:1–2).

Our relationship of trust with God enables us to hear his invitations to pray and to cast our burdens on the Lord (see Ps. 55:22). We trust the God who loves and forgives us and who cares for us in the midst of all our cares. No wonder we pray! As Calvin put it, "the more generously God deals with us, gently summoning us to unburden our cares into his bosom, the less excusable are we if his splendid and incomparable benefit does not outweigh all else with us and draw us to him, so that we apply our minds and efforts zealously to prayer."

Throughout our lives, God "gently summons" us to lay all our cares on him—our Creator and Redeemer. What a blessing! God deals gently with us. He invites us to entrust all that burdens us—all our cares—to him. Nothing is more important than God's continually drawing us into his presence through prayer and inviting us to cast all our cares on the One who loves us utterly and forever. May we zealously pray to our God!

REFLECTION QUESTION: When are times that you responded to God's call to pray and cast your cares on the Lord?

Praying for the Whole Church

Psalm 25:16–22

In Calvin's view, both Old Testament Israel and the New Testament Christian church are the people of God. Wherever the Old Testament mentioned Israel, Calvin would apply the verse to the church.

So when the psalmist prayed, "Redeem Israel, O God, out of all its troubles" (Ps. 25:22), Calvin wrote in response, "By the word *redeem*, which he here employs, we may infer that the Church was at that time oppressed with hard bondage." Israel is called "the Church."

Calvin went on to interpret this further when he wrote that "every individual, deeply affected by a sense of the public calamities which befall the Church at large, should unite with all the others in lamentation before God." Just as the psalmist identified himself as being part of Israel, so "all the afflictions and wrongs which he endured were common to himself with them."

In the same way, said Calvin, "we ought to regard it as of the greatest importance, that in accordance with this rule, every one of us, in bewailing his private miseries and trials, should extend his desires and prayers to the whole Church."

We have our own trials and troubles. We "take [them] to the Lord in prayer." But beyond praying for ourselves, we should also be praying—fervently—for the whole church. We are members of the body of Christ, and we share in the joys and sorrows that the church and all its members experience (see 1 Cor. 12:26–27).

We pray for God to redeem the church in the midst of all its troubles!

Prayer Point: Include the church in your prayers regularly.

G RANT, Almighty God, that as we are at this day tossed here and there by so many troubles, and almost all things in the world are in confusion, so that wherever we turn our eyes, nothing but thick darkness meets us,—O grant that we may learn to surmount all obstacles, and to raise our eyes by faith above the world, so that we may acknowledge that governed by thy wonderful counsel is everything that seems to us to happen by chance, in order that we may seek thee, and know that help will be ready for us through thy mercy whenever we humbly seek the pardon of our sins, through Christ Jesus our Lord.—Amen.

Wait for the Lord

Psalm 27:7–14

I<small>T</small> is always hard for us to wait. We want things done instantly—fast food, fast service, fast results.

When we pray, we sometimes have to wait for God to answer us. This wait can stretch on for quite a while. While we wait, we grow anxious. We may even believe that God is ignoring our prayer or turning a deaf ear to us.

But the psalmist urges us to wait. "Wait for the L<small>ORD</small>; be strong, and let your heart take courage; wait for the L<small>ORD</small>!" he says (Ps. 27:14).

We can wait, because we trust God. God hears and will answer our prayers, no matter what the "wait time" may be. Calvin captured this when he wrote, "If, with minds composed to this obedience, we allow ourselves to be ruled by the laws of divine providence, we shall easily learn to persevere in prayer and, with desires suspended, patiently to wait for the Lord." We trust God's providential care for us as he guides and directs us. So we patiently "wait for the Lord."

"Then," Calvin continued, "we shall be sure that, even though he does not appear, he is always present to us, and will in his own time declare how he has never had ears deaf to the prayers that in men's eyes he seems to have neglected. This, then, will be an ever-present consolation: that, if God should not respond to our first requests, we may not faint or fall into despair." God's constant presence, as we pray, comforts us. His timing is the best timing . . . so we wait for the Lord!

PRAYER **P**OINT: Pray that God will help you to wait patiently for him to answer your prayers, even when waiting is difficult.

Afflictions Lead Us to Pray

Psalm 30

A BASIC part of being a disciple of Jesus Christ is responding to Jesus's words. "If any want to become my followers, let them deny themselves and take up their cross daily and follow me" (Luke 9:23). Being a Christian means turning away from your self-interests and claims on your own life and instead following Jesus's word and will for you. To do so is to take up your "cross," just as Jesus's own obedience led to the cross where he attained salvation for us through his death.

Our daily lives are shaped by the cross of Christ and by what this cross means for our Christian obedience. The cross shapes our prayer lives and everything else. Calvin noted this in his comments on the psalmist's words "To you, O Lord, I cried, and to the Lord I made supplication" (Ps. 30:8). Calvin wrote, "No one can give himself cheerfully to prayer, until he has been softened by the cross, and thoroughly subdued. And this is the chief advantage of afflictions, that while they make us sensible of our wretchedness, they stimulate us again to supplicate the favor of God."

Afflictions that we face in our discipleship—as we live under the cross—temper and direct us. Instead of breaking us and leading to despair, our sufferings can deepen our devotion and lead us to renewed prayer. The psalmist prayed, "Hear, O Lord, and be gracious to me! O Lord, be my helper!" (Ps. 30:10). Our will becomes obedient to God's will. In our affliction, we seek God's help to see us through our distresses. We trust him!

Prayer Point: Pray for God's help during the afflictions you face, and place your will under the will of God.

GOD IS ALWAYS WILLING TO MEET US

Psalm 32

W<small>E</small> live in a time of "instant access." Whether we are checking the latest news stories or sports scores on our phones or getting money from an ATM, we like to get what we want any time—24/7.

Instant access every day to things that are important to us is one of the perks of contemporary life. But what about what is most important to us at every hour of every day: our access to God?

Long before the world had instant accessibility to common things, people of faith had instant access to the divine—to God. The prophet Isaiah wrote, "Seek the L<small>ORD</small> while he may be found, call upon him while he is near" (Isa. 55:6). The psalmist proclaimed, "Let all who are faithful offer prayer to you; at a time of distress, the rush of mighty waters shall not reach them" (Ps. 32:6). To Calvin, this verse meant that "it is never out of season, indeed, to seek God, for every moment we need his grace, and he is always willing to meet us."

We can access God through prayer in all our seasons—and in all our minutes. We can seek God and pray to him in our distress, as well as in all other instances of our lives. This is our great comfort and joy. God is always willing to meet us! There is no time or situation when God closes himself off from our prayers. We can trust that whenever we cry for his help, God hears—and answers our prayers. Rejoice; God meets us!

R<small>EFLECTION</small> Q<small>UESTIONS:</small> When have you been aware that you can approach God at any time? What are the special times in your life when you have prayed and experienced God's answer to your prayer?

CALL ON ME

Psalm 50:7–15

In one of the great verses about prayer, God says, "Call on me in the day of trouble; I will deliver you, and you shall glorify me" (Ps. 50:15).

Calvin notes that this verse has three parts: "first an injunction to prayer, then a promise of its being answered, and afterwards a call to thanksgiving." This summarizes our own experience with prayer, as well.

The immediate call of this verse is for us to pray "in the day of trouble." But, said Calvin, "not with the understanding that we are to pray only then, for prayer is a duty incumbent upon us every day, and every moment of our lives." We are to call on God at all times and in all places. This is our great invitation to invocation.

When we call on God, we will experience his deliverance. Through unexpected means, God can rescue and save us in ways that we do not anticipate or imagine. God answers our calls with what we need most: salvation and deliverance from our troubles.

Our response is to glorify him. We realize that he is the one who has brought us through all our troubles. We called, God delivered us, and now we give all praise and glory to the Lord! Rather than focusing on ourselves, we rejoice in the God who rescues us in power and love.

This invitation to call on God, with the assurance that he will answer and help, is the first thing about prayer that should impress us. When we receive his answer and help, we praise God and God alone!

REFLECTION QUESTION: Reflect on those times when, in the midst of need, you called on God and experienced his rescue and help. In what ways did you respond by praising and glorifying God?

GOD PARDONS

Psalm 51

PSALM 51 is one of the most poignant prayers in Scripture. A penitential psalm, it seeks God's pardon and forgiveness for sins that the psalmist has committed. He cannot simply forget these sins. He confesses, "I know my transgressions, and my sin is ever before me" (v. 3). He needs nothing less than God's full pardon and forgiveness. He prays, "Wash me thoroughly from my iniquity, and cleanse me from my sin" (v. 2) and "Wash me, and I shall be whiter than snow" (v. 7).

Confession of sin is the necessary step here. The psalmist confesses his sin against God—that he has "done what is evil in your sight, so that you are justified in your sentence and blameless when you pass judgment" (v. 4). Through confession, we rebuke ourselves and seek relief from our fear, shame, and despair.

Calvin said that, "provided the saints bemoan their sins, chastise themselves, and immediately return to themselves, God pardons them." This was true for the psalmist and is true for us. When we sin, we sin against God. Only God has the power—and the mercy (see v. 1)—to forgive. When God pardons us, our transgressions are blotted out (see vv. 1, 9) and we are cleansed (see v. 2). God's pardon brings us reconciliation with him, through Jesus Christ who died for our sin and who makes God's pardon possible.

Pardon begins with our confession of sin—with our deeply honest recognition of our offense against God and others. Then we can pray, "Restore to me the joy of your salvation" (v. 12). Because of God's steadfast love (see v. 1), we are pardoned!

PRAYER POINT: Spend time acknowledging and confessing your sin. Receive God's pardon.

Rely on God's Providence in Prayer

Psalm 55:16–23

A COMFORTING promise regarding prayer is found in the psalmist's words "Cast your burden on the LORD, and he will sustain you; he will never permit the righteous to be moved" (Ps. 55:22). This verse contains a promise that we find throughout Scripture—that we can give our cares and troubles to God, because he supports and cares for us in ways that keep us safe and steady and that provide for our needs.

But Calvin notes that our prayers should not be simply recitations of our "wants" to God. We should not grow anxious or clamor before God—which leads us to sometimes even "dictate" how the Almighty should answer our prayers. This goes against our loving relationship with the God in whom we have faith and whom we trust to meet our needs according to his purposes for us. Calvin said, "It is not enough that we make application to God for the supply of our wants. Our desires and petitions must be offered up with a due reliance upon his providence. . . . Acknowledge the past goodness of the Lord to have been such, that you ought to hope in his kindness for the future."

We rely on God's providence when we present our needs and desires to him, and we rest content with his ways of answering our prayers—whatever they may be! We can do this with confidence when we remember the ways that God has been good to us in the past and the ways in which his ongoing guidance sustains and blesses us. And so we can hope for his kindness in the future!

PRAYER POINT: Give your burdens to God in prayer today, trusting him to sustain you and to provide for your needs. Trust that he will hear and answer your prayer.

G RANT, Almighty God, that since thou hast once stretched forth thy hand to consecrate us a people to thyself,—O grant, that thy paternal favor may perpetually shine on us, and that we may, on the other hand, strive always to glorify thy name, so that having once embraced us thou mayest continue thy goodness, until we shall at length enjoy the fulness of all blessings in thy celestial kingdom, which has been obtained for us by the blood of thine only-begotten Son.—Amen.

GOD DOES NOT FORSAKE
OR DISAPPOINT US

Psalm 55:16–23

WHEN we have to wait long for answers to our prayers, and when we cannot see any benefits or results from our waiting and praying, only faith keeps us going. Calvin said that "our faith will make us sure of what cannot be perceived by sense, that we have obtained what was expedient." We trust, in faith, that God gives us what is best. We may not perceive it, but God is working.

Calvin continued, "For the Lord so often and so certainly promises to care for us in our troubles, when they have once been laid upon his bosom. And so he will cause us to possess abundance in poverty, and comfort in affliction. For though all things fail us, yet God will never forsake us, who cannot disappoint the expectation and patience of his people."

His words remind us of the psalmist's: "Cast your burden on the LORD, and he will sustain you; he will never permit the righteous to be moved" (Ps. 55:22).

God cares for us in our troubles as we cast our burdens upon him through prayer. He will sustain us and will "never permit the righteous to be moved." So, even in poverty, we will experience abundance. Even in affliction, we will experience comfort. These things can come only from God. We may not receive the abundance and comfort that we expect. But abundance and comfort will come to us as God's grace. Outward things may fail us, yet God will not forsake or disappoint those who wait on him with patience. What a wonderful promise of prayer!

PRAYER POINT: Ask God to bless and sustain you as you wait for him to answer your prayers.

GOD NEVER FRUSTRATES OUR PRAYERS

Psalm 56

WE are all familiar with the experience of waiting for God to answer our prayers. We pray, and often wait . . . and wait . . . for God to answer.

But we continue to believe that God hears us and answers our prayer. The psalmist expressed this confidence when he prayed for the retreat of his enemies: "Then my enemies will retreat in the day when I call" (Ps. 56:9). As he said, he knew "that God is for me."

Calvin commented that while the psalmist had "no sensible evidence of their approaching destruction . . . from the firm reliance which he exercised upon the promise, he was able to anticipate the coming period, and resolved to wait for it with patience." This patience was possible because God promises to hear and answer prayers. Even if God did not answer him immediately by scattering his enemies, the psalmist was "confident that his prayers would not be disappointed: and his ground for believing this was just a conviction of the truth, that God never frustrates the prayers of his own children."

This promise is for us, too. God will not frustrate our prayers. It is often said that God answers our prayers in one of three ways: "Yes," "No," or "Not yet." Unless God answers "Yes" immediately, we have to wait. But God's answers—even if they are "No" or "Not yet"—do not frustrate us. Instead, we keep our anxieties in check and calmly await the way in which God will respond to our prayer. We can also believe that when God says "No," he gives us something better!

REFLECTION QUESTION: Reflect on times in your prayer life when God said "Yes," when he said "No," and when he said, "Not yet."

Quietly Watch for God

Psalm 59:8–10

PRAYER and hope are inextricably bound up together. We pray in hope. If we have hope, we will pray. Praying expresses our belief in God and in what he will do. When we pray, we anticipate—in faith—the hope that God will hear and answer our prayers. When we have hope—for what God is doing and what he will do—we pray to express this hope before the Lord. Without hope, prayer is dead. Without prayer, hope is pointless.

When we pray, we look for God's answers to our prayers. As the psalmist prayed, "O my strength, I will watch for you; for you, O God, are my fortress" (Ps. 59:9). Calvin captured these essentials when he wrote that "prayers are vainly cast upon the air unless hope be added, from which we quietly watch for God as from a watchtower."

We are to watch quietly for God's answers to our prayers. Yet sometimes we do not recognize these answers. As a man was falling from a building, he prayed, "O Lord, rescue me!" Then he grabbed hold of a flagpole. He next prayed, "Never mind, Lord. I grabbed this flagpole!" Of course, the flagpole was the answer to his prayer. But the man missed this!

As we watch quietly for God's answers to our prayers, let us be alert to the ways that he may—unexpectedly!—provide them. God's Spirit can give us eyes to see ways in which God works to answer our prayers through events, people, and many other sources.

PRAYER POINT: Pray for God to give you the Holy Spirit to be able to see his answers to your prayers.

Untiring Earnestness

Psalm 86:1–7

PSALM 86 is a prayer that seeks God's help against enemies. The psalmist has great need for preservation and safety (see v. 1). He prays because he is God's servant and trusts in God. God is his only help. "You are my God," acknowledges the psalmist (v. 2); and then comes his deep prayer: "Be gracious to me, O Lord, for to you do I cry all day long" (v. 3).

In the face of deep needs, the psalmist makes continual prayer—his prayers are offered "all day long." Many times during those dangerous days, he prays for deliverance, safety, help, and hope. He can do nothing else but pray to God for mercy, since his life is fully devoted to God and founded on trust in God.

This is not a "one-and-done" prayer. The psalmist does not make a single prayer and then stop praying. Calvin says that "the inspired suppliant" (the psalmist) "not only represents himself as crying, but as persevering in doing so." He prays continually, all through the day. This teaches us that the psalmist "was not discouraged at the first or second encounter, but continued in prayer with untiring earnestness."

Do we pursue prayer this way? Do we pray to God by uttering a prayer and then forgetting about it? Do we pray earnestly to God just once, and leave it at that? Our prayers should show "untiring earnestness." We pray and keep on praying. We show our seriousness when we are "untiring." We continue to put our trust in God, who hears and answers prayers!

REFLECTION QUESTION: Recall times when you have prayed continually—what were the results?

TIMES FOR PRAYER

Psalm 88:8–18

W E all know we can pray at any time. Sometimes we pray in times of danger, anxiety, or indecision, or when we are thankful or grateful. When the Spirit moves us, we pray. This is the freedom of prayer. God hears us any day, any time.

But our freedom to pray also needs discipline. There are times when we may not feel like praying at all. Our freedom to pray leads us to be inactive in prayer. We may need help with moving toward prayer—may need to be "goaded" toward it, as Calvin says.

In this light, Calvin goes on to say, "It is fitting each one of us should set apart certain hours for this exercise. Those hours should not pass without prayer, and during them all the devotion of the heart should be completely engaged in it. These are: when we arise in the morning, before we begin daily work, when we sit down to a meal, when by God's blessing we have eaten, when we are getting ready to retire." Mornings, meals, and nights—these, suggest Calvin, are times for regular prayer, which reflect the rhythm of our lives.

The psalmist says, "Every day I call on you, O LORD; I spread out my hands to you" (Ps. 88:9). Prayer was a normal and natural phenomenon of living for him. He says, "I, O LORD, cry out to you; in the morning my prayer comes before you" (v. 13).

Pray both at set times and at any time. Most importantly, take time to pray!

REFLECTION QUESTION: Examine your prayer life and the times when you pray. What disciplines do you need in order to set specific times to pray?

CALLING ON GOD'S NAME

Psalm 91

P SALM 91 is a great expression of trust in the assurance we have that God protects us throughout our lives. He delivers us from the dangers of life—whatever they may be. The images in this psalm are ancient, but they still speak to us and assure us today. We entrust our safety to God.

We express our trust in God when we call on him in prayer. God says, "Those who love me, I will deliver; I will protect those who know my name. When they call to me, I will answer them; I will be with them in trouble, I will rescue them and honor them" (vv. 14–15). He is with us and rescues us.

We may say, Calvin notes, that we believe in God's providence. We are aware, theologically, that he protects and guides us. But the true expression of that belief comes through our prayers. Prayer turns faith into words and actions. Calvin wrote that the psalmist "now shows more clearly what was meant by trusting in God, or placing our love and delight in him. For that affection and desire which is produced by faith, prompts us to call upon his name." Faith breaks into prayer!

Calvin rightly continued, "Believers will never be exempt from troubles and embarrassments. God does not promise them a life of ease and luxury, but deliverance from their tribulations." This is really our most important and blessed gift. We lay hold of God's protecting providence and grace when we call on him. God answers and rescues us. He shows us salvation (see v. 16)!

PRAYER POINT: Make it a point to pray for God's protection and to thank him for your ongoing safety and salvation.

G RANT, Almighty God, since we have already entered in hope upon the threshold of our eternal inheritance, and know that there is a certain mansion for us in heaven after Christ has been received there, who is our head, and the first-fruits of our salvation: Grant, I say, that we may proceed more and more in the course of thy holy calling until at length we reach the goal, and so enjoy that eternal glory of which thou affordest us a taste in this world, by the same Christ our Lord.—Amen.

GOD DEALS IN GREAT
TENDERNESS TOWARD US

Psalm 102:1–2

W E can see God as judge: as the divine, holy, righteous one who has every right to punish us for our sins—to leave us to face the consequences for breaking his law and for living contrary to his will for us.

Yet Jesus Christ absorbed our sin as the sinless Son of God who died on our behalf (see Rom. 4:25). In Christ, our sin is forgiven, and we receive justification and salvation through his death and resurrection (see Rom. 5:1–11).

Now we can approach God—not as our judge, but as the one who is "for us" and who loves us with eternal love (see Rom. 5:8; 8:31, 34). This makes all the difference for our prayers! We can pray, "Answer me" (Ps. 102:2). As Calvin commented, "When God permits us to lay open before him our infirmities without reserve, and patiently bears with our foolishness, he deals in a way of great tenderness towards us. To pour out our complaints before him after the manner of little children would certainly be to treat his Majesty with very little reverence, were it not that he has been pleased to allow us such freedom. . . . [Now] the weak, who are afraid to draw near to God, may understand that they are invited to him with such gentleness as that nothing may hinder them from familiarly and confidently approaching him."

God deals with us in great tenderness. This is our joy and hope. We pray confidently, with the assurance that God lovingly hears and answers the prayers of his children!

REFLECTION QUESTION: What difference does it make for your prayers to realize that God desires to treat you with great tenderness?

PROMISES GRANTED THROUGH PRAYERS
Psalm 102:12–17

THERE are two dimensions to the way God chooses to work.

One is by directly working out his purposes—in history, in the church, and in our own lives. In this dimension, God sovereignly accomplishes his will on earth. The other is through the prayers of his people, as they make supplications and requests to him so that he will affect what happens in their lives. In this dimension, he uses prayers *about* his sovereign purposes as a means of working out those purposes in the first place.

We see the first dimension in play in Psalm 102, as the psalmist praises God as the Lord who is "enthroned forever" and will "build up Zion" (vv. 12, 16). All human powers bow before the supreme power of God, whose name "endures to all generations" (see v. 12).

The second dimension comes in as God regards and hears the prayers of his people: "He will regard the prayer of the destitute, and will not despise their prayer" (v. 17). Calvin notes that in order to "stir up true believers to greater earnestness in prayer, he promises that what he has purposed to do of his own good pleasure, he will grant in answer to their requests."

Theologically, the two dimensions of what God "has purposed to do" take place through the prayers of people who petition him. Prayer is crucial to the outworking of God's will and purposes throughout the earth, in the church, and in the lives of his people. We pray, petitioning God according to our needs, and we trust him to answer our prayers in accordance with his will.

Recognizing this should give our prayers added meaning and importance. Our prayers are means by which God works out divine purposes. God's promises are granted through our prayers. What could be more important than this!

PRAYER POINT: Make specific reference to God's will and purposes as you pray for what is deepest in your heart.

48

As Children Unburdening Their Troubles

Psalm 103:6–14

THE relationship that children have with their parents is one of the deepest relationships of life. Children depend on their parents in many ways—even for their own existence. The personal relationship of love and trust that we have with our parents when we are children is a sustaining relationship that helps us to shape our identity and security. We turn to our parents in times of trouble, seeking their comfort, guidance, and help.

Even more important is our relationship with God. God's parental love and help is a constant theme throughout Scripture. In the great 103rd Psalm, the writer details the character of God—the Lord who is "merciful and gracious" (v. 8). The psalm uses parental imagery: "As a father has compassion for his children, so the LORD has compassion for those who fear him" (v. 13).

Calvin draws on this child/parent relationship as he describes prayer. He writes, "For prayer was not ordained that we should be haughtily puffed up before God, or greatly esteem anything of ours, but that, having confessed our guilt, we should deplore our distresses before him, as children unburden their troubles to their parents."

The tender relationship experienced by children who come to their parents in great need and difficulty is also the relationship that we experience as we approach God in prayer. We confess things that we have done and unburden our troubles to our heavenly parent. God's love and care for us can be trusted; he is our source of help. In prayer, we express our deep needs to the one who has "compassion for his children." Unburden your troubles to God!

PRAYER POINT: In total honesty and trust, confess your sins to God and tell him all your distresses and troubles.

FAITH IS LIFELESS WITHOUT PRAYER

Psalm 119:49–58

THERE are times when our faith seems lifeless. We cannot focus on the things of God as we should. We have a "power failure" of the spirit.

In times like these, we need to persevere in prayer, no matter how difficult it is. Regardless of what our circumstances are or how bleak our outlook is, when we pray, we put ourselves in the best position to experience a renewal of faith and devotion to God.

The psalmist is a model for us: "I implore your favor with all my heart; be gracious to me according to your promise" (Ps. 119:58). He puts his whole heart, his whole being, into prayer. He seeks God's graciousness—or mercy, as the King James Version of verse 58 puts it—believing that he will receive God's good favor because of God's promise (v. 140).

Calvin commented, "David asserts, that he still persevered in the exercise of prayer; for without prayer faith would become languid and lifeless.... The thing which we must principally and particularly request is, that he will have mercy upon us, which is the source of every other blessing."

When our faith falters, we pray. We ask for God to have mercy on us. We ask for his help. We ask for his grace. This focuses us on what is most important for us and what, as Calvin said, is "the source of every other blessing." Without prayer, faith is lifeless and has no purpose or power. Through prayer, God aids, helps, and restores us. Seek God's favor, God's grace, and God's mercy through prayer—and receive new life!

REFLECTION QUESTION: Reflect on your prayer life through the years. What has prayer meant to you?

ANXIETY LEADS US TO PRAY

Psalm 130

T HE author of Psalm 130 expresses a deep desire to be redeemed by God. This profound longing deals with the deepest realities that we know in life: our need for God to hear our prayer, for our sin to be forgiven, and for hope to be established.

In the face of these yearnings, the psalmist does the only thing he can do—he prays. "Out of the depths I cry to you, O Lord. Lord, hear my voice! Let your ears be attentive to the voice of my supplications!" (vv. 1–2). God's saints, said Calvin, experience "huge torments," and so they call on God. As he went on to say, "Great anxiety should kindle in us the desire to pray."

Prayer invokes God; it seeks God's help regarding the deep things of life. When faced with the need for salvation, for sin to be pardoned, and for a confident expectation of experiencing God's steadfast love and redemption (see vv. 7–8), the psalmist prays—and so do we.

We pray in the midst of life's grimmest circumstances. When there is nowhere else to turn, when we need help in order to do what we cannot do for ourselves, we pray. When we wait and watch for the Lord (see vv. 5–6), we pray. Anxiety leads us to pray.

As was the case for the psalmist, when we pray, we find that our hope is kindled. This hope rests in who God is—the God of steadfast love—and in his "great power to redeem" (v. 7). Our anxieties are met by the God who redeems us and gives us hope in Jesus Christ!

REFLECTION QUESTION: Recall the times when you were most anxious. For what did you pray?

In Adversity, Pray!

Psalm 143

ADVERSITIES come to us. We experience them in many ways, often without knowing why they come upon us. But they do. And, no matter the nature of the adversities, we need to face them.

The best way for us to face adversity is to pray. When the psalmist was in a desperate situation before his enemies, he was confronting severe adversity. So he prayed, "Hear my prayer, O LORD; give ear to my supplications in your faithfulness; answer me in your righteousness. Do not enter into judgment with your servant, for no one living is righteous before you" (Ps. 143:1–2). He knew that his only help lay in praying to God. He asked God to hear and help him, not to judge him. He prayed for forgiveness and pardon.

Calvin commented, "When overtaken by adversity, we are ever to conclude that it is a rod of correction sent by God to stir us up to pray. Although he is far from taking pleasure in our trials, it is certain that our sins are the cause of his dealing towards us with this severity. . . . We must pray for the pardon of our sins."

Whether we think that our adversities arise from our specific actions or not, we are sinful people who need God's forgiveness and pardon—especially when we face great challenges. We have to move through our adversities. But first we must make sure that our relationship with God is not marred by sin. And so we pray for pardon.

We are not exempt from adversities. But we need to face them in a state of being forgiven by God!

PRAYER POINT: Spend time in prayer, confessing your sins and asking God's pardon.

G RANT, Almighty God, since thou settest before us so clear a mirror of thy wonderful providence and of thy judgments on thine ancient people, that we may also be surely persuaded of our being under thy hand and protection:— Grant, that relying on thee, we may hope for thy guardianship, whatever may happen, since thou never losest sight of our safety, so that we may invoke thee with a secure and tranquil mind. May we so fearlessly wait for all dangers amidst all the changes of this world, that we may stand upon the foundation of thy word which never can fail; and leaning on thy promises may we repose on Christ, to whom thou hast committed us, and whom thou hast made the shepherd of all thy flock. Grant that he may be so careful of us as to lead us through this course of warfare, however troublesome and turbulent it may prove, until we arrive at that heavenly rest which he has purchased for us by his own blood.—Amen.

Prayer Shows God Is Our Faithful Guardian

Psalm 145:8–21

P SALM 145 is a great psalm that praises God's greatness and goodness. God's people praise the God whose "greatness is unsearchable" (v. 3).

One of the causes for praising God's goodness that this psalm mentions is that he is "near to all who call on him" (v. 18), for he "hears their cry, and saves them" (v. 19). Calvin noted that this "last clause—*he will save them*—is also added by way of correction, to make us aware how far, and for what end God answers the prayers of his people, namely, to evidence in a practical manner that he is the faithful guardian of their welfare."

Of all the things that we need in life, God's protection and watchful care are surely among the most important. We know that we live by God's sustaining providence. God gives us life and breath each day. We also know that we live in a dangerous world in which many perils and calamities can come upon us. So much is outside our control. No matter how diligently we try to be safe and to protect ourselves, we need more than our own efforts.

God answers our prayers, throughout our lives, to be a "faithful guardian" of our welfare. He saves us, helps us, protects us, and enables us to live in safety—so that we can praise and serve him. Our prayers are answered so that life can continue and so that we can say with the psalmist, "My mouth will speak the praise of the LORD" (v. 21). God is our guardian!

REFLECTION QUESTION: In what ways have you experienced God's protection and safety in your life? Do you regularly praise God for this help and for being your guardian?

THOSE WHOSE CAUSE IS JUST

Isaiah 10:1–4

W E all have needs. But the needs of some are greater than those of others. Any look at society shows this to be true. While those who possess plenty of life's resources still have their own needs, many more people are poor and lack even the basic resources for life—clothing, shelter, food.

The Old Testament is especially strong in showing God's care for the distressed. This includes widows, orphans, immigrants, and the poor—a quartet of those whose sufferings concern God. He will judge oppressors when they "write oppressive statues, to turn aside the needy from justice and to rob the poor of my people of their right, that widows may be your spoil, and that you may make the orphans your prey!" (Isa. 10:1–2). In short, said the psalmist, "I know that the LORD maintains the cause of the needy, and executes justice for the poor" (Ps. 140:12).

According to Calvin, "just as God causes his sun to shine alike upon the good and the evil [Matt. 5:45], so he does not despise the weeping of those whose cause is just and whose distresses deserve to be relieved."

The needs of those who are in distress should always be on our hearts when we pray. God hears the cries of those whose cause is just. We, too, should support people with just causes and those who are in deep distress. We offer prayers on their behalf and express our deep concern for them through action. God wants us to do no less!

REFLECTION QUESTION: What are ways in which your prayers for those who have just causes can lead you to act on their behalf?

Opening Our Hearts before God

Isaiah 63:15–19

W E can conceive of prayer in many ways. We can think about it theologically and define its meaning. Or we can focus on the benefits that we believe we gain from it. Or we can consider it to be connecting with the divine beyond ourselves.

But something very basic about prayer emerges in a prayer of penitence in the book of Isaiah. Addressing God, the prophet says, "You, O Lord, are our father; our Redeemer from of old is your name" (v. 16).

In his comments on this verse, Calvin wrote about the basic nature of prayer: "God permits us to reveal our hearts familiarly before him; for prayer is nothing else than the opening up of our heart before God; as the greatest alleviation is, to pour our cares, distresses, and anxieties into his bosom. 'Roll thy cares on the Lord,' says David. (Ps. [37:5])."

As we converse with God in prayer, we communicate with him not only in words but also from the depths of our hearts. We reveal to him what is in our hearts, as a child does to a parent. When we open our hearts before him, we "pour" those things that mean the most to us—our "cares, distresses, and anxieties"—into the intimacy and security of our loving God.

This is what we need most in prayer—to be able to open our hearts to God and experience his caring tenderness for us. The One who knows us best loves us most. In prayer we make ourselves known to God—including all that afflicts us in the very depths of our being.

Reflection Question: Do you always open your heart and share your deepest concerns during prayer?

How God Listens to Us

Isaiah 65:17–25

Do you see, around you, what Calvin called the "visible fruit of our prayers"? Does it appear, as Calvin also said, "that God is so ready to render assistance"? It doesn't always seem that we are able to answer "yes" to these questions, does it?

Yet God promised Isaiah that "before they call I will answer, while they are yet speaking I will hear" (Isa. 65:24). God promises to answer us—even while we are speaking our prayers!

Calvin responded to these questions and God's promise by saying that, "though it becomes fully evident that we have been heard when the event actually proves it, yet God does not in the meantime overlook us; for he does not permit us to faint, but supports us by the power of his Spirit, that we may wait for him patiently." The power of God's Spirit enables us to wait patiently for God's full answer to our prayers and helps us to believe that God is not overlooking us during our waiting period.

Calvin went on to say that "there are two ways in which God listens to us; first, when he renders assistance openly; and secondly, when he aids us by the power of his Spirit, that we may not sink under the weight of afflictions." We do experience quick and direct answers to our prayers. Sometimes we are really startled by how rapidly God's answers appear!

But as we wait for his answers, however they appear, God's Spirit continues to help us. The Spirit gives us patience and hope so that "we may not sink" as we wait. God does listen to us!

Prayer Point: Pray daily for God's Spirit to strengthen and nurture you as you wait for God's answers to your prayers.

Prayer Is the Fruit of Repentance

Jeremiah 29:10–14

T HROUGH a letter from the prophet Jeremiah, God spoke to the people of Israel who were exiled in Babylon, promising them that when seventy years of exile were ended, he would bring the people back to their homeland (see Jer. 29:10). On top of that, he promised that "then when you call upon me and come and pray to me, I will hear you" (v. 12). What a promise!

This promise is significant because it indicates that the people will have faith that will lead them to pray to God. Part of this faith involves the people's repentance for their sin. Calvin notes that, "no doubt, prayer is the fruit of repentance, for it proceeds from faith; and repentance is the gift of God. And further, we cannot call on God rightly and sincerely except by the guidance and teaching of the Holy Spirit."

Theologically, Calvin always stressed that we do not "repent" and then have "faith." This would turn repentance into a "work" that humans carry out in order to gain faith.

Instead, Calvin believed that repentance expresses the faith that God gives us as a gift of grace. We repent as a sign of our faith. Repentance "proceeds from faith" and itself is a "gift of God."

We are moved to pray by the work of the Holy Spirit. The Spirit, who gives us faith, leads us to repentance and prayer. Through repentance, we confess our sin and walk into a new way of living—one that is in accordance with God's will. Express your repentance through prayer!

Reflection Question: Think of times when you have repented of sin. Did your repentance lead you to pray to God?

GROUNDED IN GOD'S PROMISES

Jeremiah 33:1–9

T HROUGHOUT the Bible, God promises to hear and answer prayers. Prayer was central to Israel. Jesus was supremely a person of prayer. The early church recognized that its life was sustained by God's providential direction and his answers to the church's prayers.

So it is for us today. Our Christian lives are full of prayer— or should be! We pray and receive God's promises that our prayers are heard and answered. Very simply, God promised Jeremiah, "Call to me and I will answer you" (Jer. 33:3). That promise was true for Jeremiah, and it is true for all Christian believers throughout the New Testament. It is a promise made to us today. Prayer is grounded in God's promises.

Calvin struck this note when he wrote that "our prayers depend upon no merit of ours, but their whole worth and hope of fulfillment are grounded in God's promises, and depend upon them, so that they need no other support, nor do they look about up and down, hither and thither." We do not cause God to answer our prayers, nor do we deserve for him to answer our prayers. God answers our prayers because he has promised to answer them, and through his answers he expresses his providential love for us.

This promise is our great comfort. Our prayers do not depend on us; they depend on God. God invites us to pray, commands us to pray, and grounds our prayers in his everlasting love for us as his children. We look to God's promise to hear and answer us. This is our great blessing!

REFLECTION QUESTION: What is the importance of realizing that our prayers are grounded in God's promises?

G RANT, Almighty God, since every perfect gift comes from thee, and since some excel others in intelligence and talents, yet as no one has anything of his own, but as thou deignest to distribute to man a measure of thy gracious liberality,—Grant that whatever intelligence thou dost confer upon us, we may apply it to the glory of thy name. Grant also, that we may acknowledge in humility and modesty what thou hast committed to our care to be thine own; and may we study to be restrained by sobriety, to desire nothing superfluous, never to corrupt true and genuine knowledge, and to remain in that simplicity to which thou callest us. Finally, may we not rest in these earthly things, but learn rather to raise our minds to true wisdom, to acknowledge thee to be the true God, and to devote ourselves to the obedience of thy righteousness; and may it be our sole object to devote and consecrate ourselves entirely to the glory of thy name throughout our lives, through Jesus Christ our Lord.—Amen.

Praying in Faith and Humility

Jeremiah 36:1–8

JEREMIAH dictated God's message to Baruch, who recorded his words on a scroll. This was read to the people of Judah (see Jer. 36:6). "It may be," said the prophet, "that their plea will come before the LORD, and that all of them will turn from their evil ways" (v. 7). Perhaps the people would be struck by their sin and would turn away from lives that were evil in God's sight.

Calvin commented that here we see the nature of prayer—"that it rises and that it falls." For "in prayer two things are necessary—faith and humility: by faith we rise up to God, and by humility we lie prostrate on the ground. This is the reason why Scripture often says that prayer ascends, for we cannot pray as we ought unless we raise upwards our minds; and faith, sustained by promises, elevates us above all the world. Thus then prayer is raised upwards by faith; but by humility it falls down on the earth; for fear ought to be connected with faith. And as faith in our hearts produces alacrity by confidence, so also conscience casts us down and lays us prostrate."

This puts it simply for us, doesn't it? We lift our hearts in faith to pray to God and are sustained by his promises; we bow in humility before God as we realize our sinfulness and the seriousness of our actions. Both dimensions are crucial for us. We look to God alone for help and trust his promises. We confess our sin. Pray confidently and humbly!

PRAYER POINT: Pray to God, in deepest honesty and trust, confessing your sins and affirming your trust in God's promises of forgiveness and reconciliation.

OUT OF OUR DESPAIR COMES HOPE

Lamentations 3:1–26

T HE book of Lamentations is well named. It is filled with laments from the writer, whose life has been severely tested by the destruction of Jerusalem. His bitterness takes full expression as he hopes for God's help in the midst of his utter despair: "My soul is bereft of peace; I have forgotten what happiness is" (Lam. 3:17). He feels that God does not hear his prayers: "Though I call and cry for help, he shuts out my prayer" (v. 8). So he pours out his heart, expressing deepest misery and desolation.

But, as Calvin notes, whoever is "conscious of his own infirmity, and directs his prayer to God, will at length find a ground of hope." That ground of hope emerges as the author of Lamentations continues to write: "But this I call to mind, and therefore I have hope: The steadfast love of the LORD never ceases, his mercies never come to an end; they are new every morning; great is your faithfulness" (vv. 21–23).

Out of despair comes hope. God's everlasting love and faithfulness bring this hope. Calvin said, "We see then that God brings light out of darkness, when he restores his faithful people from despair to a good hope." Our despair itself draws us closer to God. We cast our whole selves on him, and then hope arises. We hold nothing back; we lament to God about our condition. God hears, faith comes, and hope emerges!

This is our great confidence, even when life caves in: in the midst of misery, no matter how bad things get, God's steadfast love and faithfulness bring hope!

PRAYER POINT: Present all your difficulties to God. Then consciously remember that his steadfast love and faithfulness are your ground of hope.

Prayer: Our Adoration and Worship of God

Daniel 6:10–16

W E know the story of Daniel in the lions' den—perhaps from Sunday school. Daniel and his companions were taken from Jerusalem to Babylon, where they were commanded to pray to King Darius (see Dan. 6:6–9). But Daniel was a faithful Israelite, and he continued to pray to the God of Israel three times a day (see v. 10). For this, he was thrown into the lions' den. Faced with impending danger, he prayed to God and praised God.

Calvin wrote, "We know the principal sacrifice which God requires, is to call upon his name. For we hereby testify him to be the author of all good things; next we shew forth a specimen of our faith; then we fly to him, and cast all our cares into his bosom, and offer him our prayers. . . . Therefore, prayer constitutes the chief part of our adoration and worship of God."

Our worship includes prayer. When we pray, we recognize by faith that God has given us all good things. We "fly" to God and cast all our cares on the one who loves us. Through prayer, we worship and adore God.

It is easy to think of prayer only in terms of asking God for what we want. But praising God, remembering his benefits, and being thankful are key ingredients of prayer. We focus on who God is and what he has done, not solely on our own petitions and requests. Praise and adoration bring us into the presence of God, where we share an intimate fellowship with our Creator and Redeemer. Praise God!

Prayer Point: Practice making praise and adoration major parts of your prayers.

Prayer Is the Chief Exercise of Faith

Daniel 9:1–10

D ANIEL was a person of prayer. In the midst of the dangers and difficulties that he and his companions faced in Babylon, Daniel practiced prayer regularly and fervently: "Then I turned to the Lord God, to seek an answer by prayer and supplication with fasting and sackcloth and ashes. I prayed to the LORD my God" (Dan. 9:3–4).

Calvin commented on Daniel's experience: "God does not here promise his children earthly blessings, but eternal life, and while they grow torpid and cast aside all care and spiritual concern, he urges them the more earnestly to prayer. For what benefit do God's promises confer on us, unless we embrace them by faith? But prayer is the chief exercise of faith. . . . For the true proof of faith is the assurance when we pray that God will really perform what he has promised us."

Our prayers do not assure "earthly blessings." They point us, most importantly, toward eternal life. This blessing we receive by faith. Prayer is a venture of faith—indeed, said Calvin, "the chief exercise of faith." Our prayers express our faith in God, who hears and answers prayer. Through our prayers, we say that we believe God will really perform his promises that we find in Scripture. We affirm that we believe these promises—those for the world, those for the church, and those for our own lives. In prayer, we turn all things over to the Lord. We trust his loving care and guidance to sustain us.

May we, like Daniel, be people of prayer who express our faith!

PRAYER POINT: In prayer, ask God to strengthen your faith in his promises.

Put Away All Self-Assurance

Daniel 9:15–19

In prayer, we completely empty ourselves so that we can be filled by God.

We pray to God on the basis of his desire for humanity to live in a relationship of love and trust with our Creator. We pray in order to speak to God and listen to God. We know that this vital relationship is necessary for our lives. As Christians, we approach God through Jesus Christ, our Lord and Savior. Through Christ's merit and the power of the Holy Spirit, we come before God—realizing that we come not by our own merit or power. Daniel prayed, "We do not present our supplication before you on the ground of our righteousness, but on the ground of your great mercies" (Dan. 9:18). So we empty ourselves in order to be filled by God.

We come before God in complete humility and with a focus on God's glory—never on our own. Calvin emphasized this when he wrote, "Anyone who stands before God to pray, in his humility giving glory completely to God, [must] abandon all thought of his own glory, cast off all notion of his own worth, in fine, put away all self-assurance—lest if we claim for ourselves anything, even the least bit, we should become vainly puffed up, and perish at his presence."

Put away all self-assurance and, in prayer, rely only on God. We can claim no might or power to achieve things on our own. In prayer there is no room for pride or vanity. We can only throw ourselves on God's mercy and love!

REFLECTION QUESTION: Think of your prayers and of times when you have been too "self-assured" while praying—when you have put emphasis on what you can do instead of relying solely on what God can do.

Touched with True Penitence

Daniel 10:10–14

SOMETIMES in our prayers, in our rush to let God know what we want to say, we neglect to focus on who he is and who we are.

We approach God in prayer because he graciously invites and commands us to "Call on me" (Ps. 50:15). We come to him as children come to their parents, pouring out our hearts and desires to our God.

As we do, we should also recognize that we pray to God because he is God—and we are not! We trust and depend on him. We recognize his sovereignty and lordship. We believe that our only hope is for God to hear our prayers and answer them according to his will. We remember 1 John 5:14: "If we ask anything according to his will, he hears us."

But true prayer, said Calvin, will also recognize what Scripture indicates about the prayers of Daniel: that "the faithful humble themselves before God, and being touched with true penitence, pour out their groans before him." God told Daniel, "Do not fear, Daniel, for from the first day that you set your mind to gain understanding and to humble yourself before your God, your words have been heard, and I have come because of your words" (Dan. 10:12). Daniel was touched with true penitence, and he humbled himself before God. He recognized who God was and who he was. He approached God with humility and reverence.

So should we. We turn from our sins, humble ourselves, and pray in penitence to God.

PRAYER POINT: Make penitence a part of your prayers as you contemplate God.

G RANT, Almighty God, that as thou hast given us thy only begotten Son to rule us, and hast by thy good pleasure consecrated him a King over us, that we may be perpetually safe and secure under his hand against all the attempts of the devil and of the whole world,—O grant, that we may suffer ourselves to be ruled by his authority, and so conduct ourselves, that he may ever continue to watch for our safety: and as thou hast committed us to him, that he may be the guardian of our salvation, so also suffer us not either to turn aside or to fall, but preserve us ever in his service, until we be at length gathered into that blessed and everlasting kingdom, which has been procured for us by the blood of thy only Son. Amen.

No Distresses Should Keep Us from Praying

Joel 2:28–32

I N a picture of the coming days, the prophet Joel portrays the pouring out of God's Spirit "on all flesh" (Joel 2:28) and the coming judgment as the "day of the LORD" (v. 31).

This is the worst situation imaginable! God's judgment is coming. But there is a promise: "Then everyone who calls on the name of the LORD shall be saved" (v. 32). Those who are saved call on "the name of the LORD"—they pray for God's help and deliverance.

However the scene that it describes may end up being fulfilled, we cannot miss the implication of this passage: there is no distress imaginable that can keep us from praying to God. No situation!

Calvin commented, "Since then God invites here the lost and the dead, there is no reason why even the heaviest distresses should preclude an access for us or for our prayers; for we ought to break through all these obstacles. The more grievous, then, our troubles are, the more confidence we ought to entertain; for God offers his grace, not only to the miserable, but also to those in utter despair."

This is the word of hope for us today. We can pray to God in the midst of the "heaviest distresses." The worse our troubles, "the more confidence" we should have in God's help. We may pray to God when we are miserable. And even if we are in "utter despair," we can (and must!) pray to God. For he gives grace to those who are in this most dire of all situations.

Let nothing deter you from praying to the God who helps!

REFLECTION QUESTION: In what ways do the worst of circumstances lead you to pray even more fervently?

The Spirit Raises Our Hearts to Heaven

Micah 3:1–4

Sometimes we treat prayer flippantly—casually—as though it is just as a process we go through without focusing our hearts on God. These can be dangerous times. Micah warned government officials that if they oppressed the people, didn't practice justice, and hated good and loved evil (see Micah 3:2), "then they will cry to the Lord, but he will not answer them; he will hide his face from them at that time, because they have acted wickedly" (v. 4). This was a truly serious warning!

Images like this in Scripture serve to caution us. They also encourage us to pursue their opposite—what would it be like not to love wickedness and not to oppress people, but to live as God prescribes and desires? Calvin took this approach when he wrote that "except one is guided by the Spirit of God, he cannot pray from the heart. And we know that it is the peculiar office of the Spirit to raise up our hearts to heaven: for in vain we pray, except we bring faith and repentance: and who is the author of these but the Holy Spirit?"

The Holy Spirit raises our hearts to heaven, enabling us to pray as we should. In the Spirit, we pray with hearts that are truly focused on God and are turned away from wickedness and our own bad actions. We treat prayer seriously, praying in faith and repentance as we call on God. We ask God's Spirit to guide our hearts and lives so that we can be humble before God.

Prayer Point: Examine your heart and actions to see if you are focused on God and living as he desires. Pray for God's Spirit to lift your heart to God, in true humility and repentance.

Unburdening Our Cares, Griefs, and Anxieties

Habakkuk 1:1–4

THE book of Habakkuk begins with the prophet bitterly crying to God. He complains, "O LORD, how long shall I cry for help, and you will not listen? Or cry to you 'Violence!' and you will not save?" (Hab. 1:2). We can scarcely imagine a deeper, angrier, or more desperate prayer.

Sometimes we feel like speaking to God in these terms. We have deep complaints, anger, and desperate feelings to voice. They are so strong that we can express them to only one person: God. Are we wrong to do so? Should we be more "restrained" in what we say to God when we pray?

Calvin spoke about this when he wrote, "Wherefore do we pray, but that each of us may unburden his cares, his griefs, and anxieties, by pouring them into the bosom of God? Since, then, God allows us to deal so familiarly with him, nothing wrong ought to be ascribed to our prayers when we thus freely pour forth our feelings."

In prayer, we can say all things to God. We can be brutally honest with our feelings. We can express our deepest fears, anxieties, and griefs. God can withstand such prayers! For he "allows us," says Calvin, to "deal so familiarly with him." We can pour our deepest troubles "into the bosom of God."

This is the best blessing that we have. God invites us into a relationship in which we can cry out even our most profoundly disturbing feelings to him. God receives our prayers—and us!

PRAYER POINT: Pray to God, unburdening all your cares, griefs, and anxieties. Trust him to hear and bless you as you experience these difficulties.

Seek a Corner, Not a Crowd

Matthew 6:5–6

Evidently it was common in Jesus's day for people to offer prayers very publicly and prominently. Jesus spoke about "hypocrites" who "love to stand and pray in the synagogues and at the street corners, so that they may be seen by others" (Matt. 6:5). Such people "have received their reward," he said. They may seem to be pious in the eyes of the crowds. But their prayers will not have an effect. The adulation of those crowds is their only "reward"!

Instead, Jesus said, "Whenever you pray, go into your room and shut the door and pray to your Father who is in secret; and your Father who sees in secret will reward you" (v. 6). Prayer is not to be a public spectacle; it is an intimate conversation between us and God.

Calvin commented that "we should rather look for a corner, than go after a crowd of people so that they may see us at prayer." Today we may not seek for crowds to hear our prayers. But Calvin cuts to the nub: Jesus is "simply putting right a vain desire for glory. This is the sum of it: whether one is alone or in company at prayer the attitude to adopt is to think of God as one's witness, as though shut off in an inside room."

Desire for glory comes in many forms. But in prayer, our only "audience" is God. God is our "witness," and we say our prayers to him. We do not pray in order to be praised by others. We pray only to our Lord!

Reflection Question: Ask yourself in what ways you may be seeking visibility and the praise of others for your faith. Think of ways that you can seek not your own glory in the eyes of others but only the glory of God.

Why Pray?

Matthew 6:7–8

J ESUS said something that, while we know it is true, might make us question why we should pray. Our Master said, "Your Father knows what you need before you ask him" (Matt. 6:8). Calvin put it this way: "If God knows what we need before we seek it, there might appear to be no benefit in prayer." So why pray?

Calvin went on to explain: "The faithful do not pray to tell God what He does not know, or urge Him to His duties, or hurry Him on when He delays, but rather to alert themselves to seek Him, to exercise their faith by meditating upon His promises, unburdening their cares by lifting themselves into His bosom, and finally to testify that from Him alone, all good for themselves and for others is hoped and asked." The purposes of prayer go far beyond simply petitioning God or asking him for what we need or desire. We seek God in prayer, meditate on his promises, unburden our cares to him, and fully acknowledge that he is the source of all good—for both us and others. Much goes on in prayer!

Calvin urged, "Keep hold of both points, then: our prayers are anticipated by Him in His freedom, yet, what we ask we gain by prayer." This keeps prayer in perspective. Why pray? God knows our needs and will meet those needs. Prayer is our means of communion with God through conversation—which includes praise, petition, and thanksgiving—and is a means by which his help comes to us. Pray!

REFLECTION QUESTION: Reflect on the wonder of God's knowing our needs and giving us a way by which we can communicate with him!

Praying for the Glory of God

Matthew 6:7–14

In today's passage, Jesus gives his disciples the Lord's Prayer as the model for how they should pray. It's a familiar prayer that we pray on a variety of occasions. The petitions that are contained in the prayer cover the needs of our lives and demonstrate how we should offer them to God.

But we need to recognize, as Calvin notes, that just as the Ten Commandments have two tables—one concerning devotion to God and the other concerning charity to others—so the Lord's Prayer has two parts: one concerning the glory of God and the other concerning our own needs. The sequence of these two parts is important. As Calvin wrote, "We shall only be adjusted to pray as we should, when we are not anxious simply for ourselves, and for our own cause, but give prior place to the glory of God, for it is quite absurd if we only take care for our own business, and neglect the kingdom of God, which is so much more important."

We pray, to God in heaven, that his name be "hallowed"—holy. We pray for his reign, or kingdom, to come and for his will to be done—here on earth. These petitions show us that God's glory is the first and foremost thing that we should pray for. Then come prayers for our daily bread, forgiveness, and safety. Before prayers for our needs are prayers for God's glory to be visible and to extend through all the earth. We live to give glory to God. Our Lord's Prayer keeps what is most important before us: the glory of God!

Reflection Question: What are some ways that we can not only pray for the glory of God but also enact or live out his glory in our lives?

G RANT, Almighty God, that since we want so many aids while in this frail life, and as it is a shadowy life, we cannot pass a moment, except thou dost continually, and at all times, supply through thy bounty what is needful,—O grant, that we may so profit by thy so many benefits, that we may learn to raise our minds upwards, and ever aspire after celestial life, to which by thy gospel thou invitest us so kindly and sweetly every day, that being gathered into thy celestial kingdom, we may enjoy that perfect felicity, which has been procured for us by the blood of thy Son, our Lord Jesus Christ. Amen.

THE GOAL OF ALL OUR PRAYERS

Matthew 6:9–13

MANY Christians end the Lord's Prayer with the traditional doxology, or praise of God, that is found in the King James Version of Matthew 6:13: "For thine is the kingdom, and the power, and the glory, for ever. Amen." (Other English translations of the Bible contain a variation of this doxology in a footnote.)

This is a fitting conclusion to the prayer that Jesus taught his disciples. It anticipates the kingdom of God, which has already begun in Jesus Christ and will come in all its fullness in the future.

Calvin saw this doxology as important. He wrote, "It was added not only to warm our hearts to press towards the glory of God, and warn us what should be the goal of all our supplications, but also to tell us that all our prayers, here set down for us, have no other foundation than God alone, in case we should put any weight upon our own merits."

Do we keep in mind that the goal of all our prayers should be God's kingdom—his reign on earth and in heaven, now and in the future? Remembering this means that our prayers will focus on the glory of God in all its fullness. Our prayers will be grounded in "God alone"—never in ourselves. We pray for our needs and desires, but we pray for them in order to honor God and serve his kingdom.

God's reign is coming! It is already here in Jesus Christ. Today, we can "live into" the kingdom of God by following Christ's purposes for the lives that we live as his disciples.

PRAYER POINT: Make praise for God's kingdom part of all your prayers and express your desire to serve his kingdom every day.

ASK FOR WHAT ACCORDS WITH GOD'S WILL

Matthew 7:7–11

O UR ultimate goal for our prayer is that our will and desires be in accord with God's will and purposes. This is first and foremost.

The famous first question of the Westminster Shorter Catechism asks, "What is the chief end of man?" The answer is, "Man's chief end is to glorify God and to enjoy him forever." This reflects biblical teaching. Our end, goal, or purpose for living is to give glory and honor to our Creator, the Lord God. All else—our wills and desires—come later. These must always be focused on and emerge from our deepest desire: to give glory to God!

Jesus promised that God gives "good things" to those who pray (Matt. 7:11). But we see from Jesus's life that his first priority was to do God's will and to give him glory (see, for example, Matthew 26:36–46). So it is for us. As Calvin put it, "Whoever wishes to approach God with confidence in his prayers, should learn to curb his heart, and ask for nothing which is not in accordance with His will."

We can be honest with God in our prayer. We can ask him for those things that are deep in our hearts and desires. But we should always express these with our overall—and deepest—desire being for what we want to concur with the will of God.

Our hearts are set on God and on doing his will. We find our most profound purpose in living for God's glory. Then, from that purpose, our prayers emerge—prayers that always ask for what accords with God's will.

REFLECTION QUESTION: What are ways in which you can keep your prayers focused first and foremost on seeking God's will?

Our Prayers Are Never Rejected

Matthew 9:27–30

O ne day, Jesus healed two blind men. They cried loudly to Jesus, "Have mercy on us, Son of David!" He asked them, "Do you believe that I am able to do this?" They said, "Yes, Lord." Jesus then touched their eyes and said, "According to your faith let it be done to you." Then, "their eyes were opened" (Matt. 9:27–30).

Concerning this story, Calvin wrote, "Though the narrative here is of a particular favour done to the two blind men, we may well take a general lesson from this utterance of Christ, that we (as long as we pray from faith) shall never suffer rejection in our prayers." This is an ongoing comfort for us. As we pray in faith, God will always hear our prayers and never refuse to answer them.

Calvin continued, "If these two men, of slight and scarcely formed faith, gained what they wished, much more today shall the faith of those men avail who come to God with the gift of the adoption of the Spirit, and in reliance upon the sacrifice of the Mediator." We who now know Jesus Christ by faith through the work of the Holy Spirit and have received the benefit of his death for us can even more clearly and directly believe that our prayers, which arise from faith, will be heard and answered by God.

We are assured, by our faith in the work of Christ and the Holy Spirit, that our prayers are never rejected. God will always hear us!

Reflection Question: What are practical benefits of believing that your prayers are never rejected by God?

OUR DAILY PRAYER

Matthew 21:1–9

WHEN Jesus entered Jerusalem on Palm Sunday, the crowds shouted, "Hosanna to the Son of David! Blessed is the one who comes in the name of the Lord! Hosanna in the highest heaven!" (Matt. 21:9), praising him with a prayer that was drawn from Psalm 118:25–26: "Save us, we beseech you, O LORD! O LORD, we beseech you, give us success! Blessed is the one who comes in the name of the LORD." "Hosanna" is a Hebrew expression that means "Save, I [or *we*] pray" or "Save, now." By saying this, the Hebrews were praying for God's help to save his people.

Calvin noted that not only "did the Spirit train . . . the ancient people [of the Old Testament] to pray daily for the reign of Christ," but the account of the triumphal entry proves that "the same rule is laid down for us nowadays." Drawing from this account, Calvin gives us what we can call "Our Daily Prayer."

We should pray daily for the reign of Christ. This is to be such a passion for us that we should pray daily to God for Christ's reign to be enacted. Jesus gave us this way to say it in the Lord's Prayer: "Thy kingdom come" (Matt. 6:10 KJV). We pray for Christ's reign and Christ's people—the church—to express God's will and purposes for the earth and for the people on it.

Our daily prayer acknowledges, said Calvin, that "this Kingdom is not set up" by humans or "sustained by their power but stands invincible by heavenly help." But we pray—and work now—for the reign of Christ to be real among us!

PRAYER POINT: Pray daily for Christ's reign throughout the earth and its people.

THE TREASURES OF PRAYER

Matthew 21:18–22

GOD's promises and our prayers are bound up together.

God is completely true and reliable. What he says, he does. What he promises, he performs. This is at the core of biblical faith. We believe in God, and we believe God. Throughout the Scriptures, when God makes promises, they are fulfilled.

When we pray, we can claim the promises God has made to people of faith and can ask him to fulfill them. Jesus put it this way: "Whatever you ask for in prayer with faith, you will receive" (Matt. 21:22).

We know God's promises from the Word of God. The Scriptures give us his promises—the greatest of which was fulfilled when God sent his Son, Jesus Christ, as the Messiah who died for the sins of the world (see 1 Cor. 15:3). As we read God's Word, we can receive God's promises as he gives them and as we pray. Calvin wrote that "we see that to us nothing is promised to be expected from the Lord, which we are not also bidden to ask of him in prayers. So true is it that we dig up by prayer the treasures that were pointed out by the Lord's gospel, and which our faith has gazed upon."

The "treasures" of prayer are presented to us through the promises of God that we find in "the Lord's gospel" and that we make our own through faith—and through our prayers.

Are the treasures of prayer coming to us? As we pray, are we expecting to receive God's promises? Are we gazing on the treasures of God, by faith?

REFLECTION QUESTION: What promises of God are especially meaningful to you? When do you pray about them?

BEGGING FROM GOD

Matthew 26:36–46

J ESUS praying in the garden of Gethsemane before he was
arrested and crucified is one of the most agonizing portraits
in Scripture. Jesus told his disciples that he was "deeply grieved,
even to death" (Matt. 26:38). In his prayer, he poignantly prayed,
"'My Father, if it is possible, let this cup pass from me; yet not
what I want but what you want'" (v. 39).

As we know, this cup of sorrow and death did not depart
from Jesus. He was arrested and crucified. But in this prayer we
see the very human Jesus submitting himself to the divine plan
and being obedient to the will of God in all things.

Calvin draws from Jesus a lesson for our own prayers: "We
see how prayers may be holy which appear to differ from the
will of God, for He does not wish us to ask always with exactness
and scruple what He has decreed, but allows us to beg from Him
what our intelligence can grasp as desirable."

This is a word of encouragement for us. We ought always
to orient our prayers toward seeking to be obedient to the
divine will. But this does not mean we cannot be honest in our
prayers—we can tell our hopes and desires to God. He will "sort
it all out," even as we "beg" him for whatever our deepest long-
ings may be.

We yield ourselves to God's will in prayer. But we also
express our own wishes in prayer. We trust that God's will and
purposes will become plain—and then, when they do, we give
ourselves to them.

PRAYER POINT: Ask God's Spirit to help you to always
be obedient to God's will, even as you express your own
desires deeply and fully in your prayer.

Grant, Almighty God, that as thou hast not only redeemed us by the blood of thy only begotten Son, but also guidest us during our earthly pilgrimage, and suppliest us with whatever is needful,—O grant, that we may not be unmindful of so many favours, and turn away from thee and follow our sinful desires, but that we may continue bound to thy service, and never burden thee with our sins, but submit ourselves willingly to thee in true obedience, that by glorifying thy name we may carry thee both in body and soul, until thou at length gatherest us into that blessed kingdom which has been obtained for us by the blood of thy Son. Amen.

ENTERING INTO PRAYER

Mark 9:14–29

A MAN brought his son to Jesus. The son was possessed by a "spirit" that convulsed him and made him unable to speak (see Mark 9:17–18). Jesus's disciples could not cast out the spirit. So the father said to Jesus, "If you are able to do anything, have pity on us and help us" (v. 22).

Jesus responded, "If you are able!—All things can be done for the one who believes" (v. 23). Immediately, the father cried out, "I believe; help my unbelief!" (v. 24). Then Jesus healed his son.

"If you are able!"—this summarizes the attitude that we sometimes have about prayer. We don't know—for certain!—whether prayer is worthwhile and whether it will help or benefit us. Is prayer worth the effort?

Calvin knew this about us. He wrote, "The first foundation of faith is to embrace the infinite power of God. The first entry into prayers is to rise above all obstacles so that we are firmly convinced that our praying will not be in vain."

Prayer is built on faith—on believing that God hears and helps us when we pray. Without faith, prayer is empty and dead. But when we believe that God's "infinite power" can help us—and that God wants to help us—then our prayer fully expresses our faith. And so we believe . . . and so we pray.

Against all obstacles, doubts, and mistrusts, we pray. We enter into prayer, trusting and believing that our prayers will "not be in vain." God desires our prayers. We cast all that is within us on God. "If you are able"—yes, God is able!

PRAYER POINT: Begin your prayers by expressing trust that God will hear and can answer them, and praise him for it.

Faith Breaks into Prayer

Mark 11:20–24

After Jesus cursed a fig tree that was not bearing figs, the disciples noticed that "the fig tree withered away to its roots" (Mark 11:20). Jesus then spoke of the power of prayer. He expressed its great power: "Have faith in God. Truly I tell you, if you say to this mountain, 'Be taken up and thrown into the sea,' and if you do not doubt in your heart, but believe that what you say will come to pass, it will be done for you. So I tell you, whatever you ask for in prayer, believe that you have received it, and it will be yours" (vv. 22–24). Jesus links prayer with faith. "Believing" is the key ingredient for prayer.

Calvin captured this when he wrote that "to have faith in God means precisely the assurance and expectation from God of whatever we need. As faith, if we have any, immediately breaks into prayer and reaches for the riches of the grace of God which are revealed in the Word, that we should enjoy them, so Christ adds prayer to faith. . . . The true test of faith lies in prayer."

Faith believes, with assurance, that through prayer God will provide what we need. Faith gives way to prayer as it reaches for the blessings of God's grace, which are revealed in the Scriptures. Indeed, said Calvin, the truest test of faith is whether it goes on to be expressed to God in prayer.

Do we pray with assurance? Do we believe as we pray? Let's commit to a deeper faith that calls on God and breaks into prayer!

Prayer Point: Express in your prayers that you believe God will hear and answer the prayers that you pray to him.

Prayers for Daily Needs

Luke 11:1–4

W E are used to planning for the future. We plan financially to anticipate our needs so that we will be prepared with the resources to meet them.

This planning has its place. But mostly we live in a basic way—day to day. We have needs each day, and each day we hope that these needs will be met.

This is how the children of Israel lived in the wilderness. God provided "manna" to feed the people. The manna came to them overnight, and God commanded that "each day the people shall go out and gather enough for that day" (Ex. 16:4). God provided for their needs day by day.

In the Lord's Prayer, Jesus commanded us to pray to God for the needs we experience each day. We pray, "Give us each day our daily bread" (Luke 11:3). We live by faith—faith that God will provide for our needs each day and will provide for our needs tomorrow as well. As Calvin put it, "We are bidden to ask only as much as is sufficient for our need from day to day, with this assurance: that as our Heavenly Father nourishes us today, he will not fail us tomorrow."

Do we live this way? When we pray for our daily needs, do we express our faith and dependence on God? We should do this daily to show that our faith is fresh and new every morning. We cannot "hoard" faith—just as the Israelites could not hoard manna. We rely and trust in God each day with the assurance that he provides for our needs today . . . and in all our tomorrows!

Prayer Point: Pray that God will help you to express your needs daily.

PERSISTENCE IN PRAYER

Luke 11:5–13

JESUS told a parable about being persistent in prayer (see Luke 11:5–8). At midnight, a man needed three loaves of bread from his friend. The friend, who was in bed, did not want to help. But because of the man's persistent requests, the friend relented. If one person will do that for another because of his persistence, how much more will God answer the prayers of those who pray—and who keep on praying!

Calvin commented, "There is no reason for the faithful to grow weary at heart, if they do not at once obtain their requests, or if what they ask for seems difficult to achieve, for, if you can put pressure on men by importunity in asking, when a man will not do a thing for you willingly, we should have no doubt that God will attend to our prayer, if we persist at it with resolution, and do not let our hearts faint through delay or difficulty."

This is a word of hope for us as we pray, is it not? God's goodness exceeds any person's goodness. If a human will help another due to his persistence, even more will God help us! Beyond that, he loves us inexpressibly. He wants to answer our prayers. Jesus said, "Ask, and it will be given you. . . . For everyone who asks receives, and everyone who searches finds, and for everyone who knocks, the door will be opened" (Luke 11:9–10).

We should not let our faith in God or in prayer collapse, nor should we grow weary, if our prayer is not answered "quickly enough." Persist in prayer!

PRAYER POINT: Make it a point to persist in prayer—continue to pray over a period of time for what is important.

Praying from Need and Desire

John 11:1–44

Jesus's raising of his friend Lazarus, in John 11, movingly shows us God's compassion and the power he has in Jesus Christ to raise the dead.

Mary and Martha, Lazarus's sisters, sent a message entreating, or praying, to Jesus for help (v. 3). Their plea, while short, was deeply felt. They looked to Jesus, knowing that only he could help. They intensely hoped for his aid. Then Lazarus died (v. 11).

Calvin noted that one of the rules of prayer is that "in our petitions we ever sense our own insufficiency, and earnestly pondering how we need all that we seek, join with this prayer an earnest—nay, burning—desire to attain it." In the story of Lazarus, he saw Mary and Martha as acting this way toward Christ. They showed that the "chief thing" is "to cast our cares and whatever troubles us into the bosom of God, that He may supply the remedy." The sisters did this, and "from Christ's love they conceive a trust to receive help." They believed. Calvin continued, "This is a perpetual rule of true prayer; for where there is God's love, there is sure and present salvation. He does not love and forsake."

We pray out of our need and desire. We look beyond ourselves for God's strong aid. We have a burning desire to receive help for our needs. Trusting that God wills to help us, we "cast our cares" into "the bosom of God." We know that, since God loves us, he will not forsake us!

Prayer Point: Pray about your deepest needs and desires. Cast yourself wholly on God, remembering his loving compassion and his power to help you.

Fly to Him

John 15:1–11

Jesus made promises to his disciples, and they are deeply meaningful to us today.

One of Jesus's most comforting promises is that "if you abide in me, and my words abide in you, ask for whatever you wish, and it will be done for you" (John 15:7).

This is a profound assurance that we have access to Christ and that our prayers are heard and answered. Calvin wrote, "Whatever those in Christ may lack, there is relief ready for their poverty, so soon as they seek it from God. This is a very useful admonition, for the Lord often lets us go hungry to train us to earnestness in prayer. If we fly to Him, we shall never lack what we ask, but He will supply us from His inexhaustible abundance with all that we need (1 Cor. 1.5)."

This may make it seem that we have free rein—that we can pray for anything we want and receive our every wish! The sky's the limit! But Jesus is clear that the prayers he is talking about spring from Christ's words and teachings that dwell in us. As Calvin said, Jesus means that "we take root in Him by faith." We pray aright when we subject "all our affections to the will of God."

But the promise is plain. When we "fly to him," we will not lack what we ask. God will supply us from the "inexhaustible abundance" of his love and care. Jesus's word assures us: God provides all that we ask . . . and need!

Reflection Question: Think about the requests you have made to God and the answers you have received. Has God provided what you have requested? Has he provided for what you need?

G RANT, Almighty God, that as we are so scattered in our pilgrimage in this world, that even a dreadful spectacle is presented to our eyes, when we see thy Church so miserably rent asunder,—O grant, that being endued with the real power of thy Spirit, and gathered into one, we may so cultivate [affectionate] kindness among ourselves, that each may strive to help another, and at the same time keep our eyes fixed on Christ Jesus; and though hard contests may await us, may we yet be under his care and protection, and so exercise patience, that having finished our warfare, we may at last enjoy that blessed rest, which thou hast promised to us, and which is laid up for us in heaven, and which has also been purchased for us by the blood of Christ thy Son, our Lord. Amen.

DON'T BE WEARIED BY DELAY

Acts 1:12–14

I MAGINE being part of the company of disciples after Jesus ascended into heaven (see Acts 1:6–11), as they waited for the coming of the Holy Spirit whom Jesus had promised (see vv. 4–5). You would be waiting for the Spirit—but, while you waited, you would also be joining with the other disciples in prayer: "All these were constantly devoting themselves to prayer, together with certain women, including Mary the mother of Jesus, as well as his brothers" (v. 14). The disciples' faith led them to pray.

This was "an exercise of their patience," Calvin said, "in that Christ kept them in suspense for a time when He could have sent the Spirit at once." The disciples experienced this, and so do we. Calvin continued, "God often delays and seems to let us languish, to teach us the habit of perseverance. The impatience of our prayers is a harmful, even a baneful, disease; so it is no surprise if God corrects it. Meanwhile as I say, He trains us to be constant in prayer. Therefore if we wish not to pray in vain let us not be wearied by delay."

Don't be wearied by delay—what an important, but difficult, message for us! Day after day, month after month we may pray . . . and wait. Our waiting can dissuade us from believing that God hears us or that he will answer. But we persevere in prayer. We trust and have faith that as we pray, God is working. Impatience can harm our faith. Through perseverance, our faith can be strengthened. Don't be wearied by God's delay!

REFLECTION QUESTION: What do you keep telling yourself over and over again as you wait for God's answer to your prayers?

WITHOUT CEASING

Romans 1:8–15

PAUL prayed often and urged others to do so as well. Prayer was foundational to Paul's life of faith, just as it is to ours.

In prayer, we bring both our needs and the needs of others before the Lord. Paul portrayed what this wide net of prayer is like when he wrote to the church at Rome: "Without ceasing I remember you always in my prayers" (Rom. 1:9). He gave believers in other churches the same message (see Eph. 1:16; Phil. 1:4). In these statements, Paul also emphasized the constancy of his prayers, which were made "without ceasing." "Pray without ceasing" was a clear directive that he gave to the church in Thessalonica (1 Thess. 5:17).

Calvin noted that "it is to prayer that the saints deliberately devote themselves, even as we see that the Lord Himself sought a place of retirement for such a purpose. At the same time, however, Paul denotes the frequency, or rather the continuance, of his habit of prayer by saying that he devoted himself to prayer *unceasingly*."

"Pray without ceasing" is an important reminder for us— all the time. Though our prayers may not always be verbal or explicit, we can maintain an attitude that helps us to pray "without ceasing." We do this when we keep God and his purposes foremost in our minds and are constantly alert for the needs of others for whom we pray—and act. Prayer is an attitude that breaks forth into words, whether silent or audible. As we look outward, we pray for others. When we look inward, we pray for ourselves. Pray without ceasing!

> REFLECTION QUESTION: What are ways in which you practice praying "without ceasing"?

The Spirit Stirs Prayers

Romans 8:26–27

WHENEVER we pray, we can thank the Holy Spirit for stirring our hearts to do so.

The Spirit and prayer are joined. Paul indicates that the work of the Holy Spirit is what makes our prayers originate. The Spirit presents our prayers and intercedes for us. Paul wrote, "The Spirit helps us in our weakness; for we do not know how to pray as we ought, but that very Spirit intercedes with sighs too deep for words" (Romans 8:26).

Calvin expanded on this to say, "The Spirit, therefore, must prescribe the manner of our praying. . . . He stirs up in our hearts the prayers which it is proper for us to address to God. . . . He affects our hearts in such a way that these prayers penetrated into heaven itself by their fervency. . . . We are bidden to knock. But no one of his own accord could premeditate a single syllable, unless God were to knock to gain admission to our souls by the secret impulse of His Spirit, and thus open our hearts to Himself."

The Spirit's work takes place before, while, and after we pray. The Spirit "has us covered"! Our impulse to pray comes from the Spirit, who opens our hearts to God. As we submit to that impulse, the Spirit leads us in fervent prayer. God hears our prayers as we "knock" on the gates of heaven (so to speak!). Then the Spirit intercedes on our behalf.

We never pray alone. The Spirit is always with us, doing for us what we cannot do for ourselves!

PRAYER POINT: In your prayers, be especially alert to ways in which the Spirit is at work—prompting you to pray and directing what you pray for—and then believe that the Spirit continues to intercede for you.

THE SPIRIT IS OUR TEACHER

Romans 8:26–27

L EFT to ourselves, we would flail and fail in prayer. We fear that we don't have the right words or can't express our emotions. Knowing that God hears us when we seek his divine will for our lives (see 1 John 5:14), we wonder whether we can turn our minds and hearts to seek his will as we pray.

But we are not left in a hopeless situation! Calvin writes that "in order to minister to this weakness, God gives us the Spirit as our teacher in prayer, to tell us what is right and temper our emotions. For, 'because we do not know how to pray as we ought, the Spirit comes to our help,' and 'intercedes for us with unspeakable groans' [Rom. 8:26]; not that he actually prays or groans but arouses in us assurance, desires, and sighs, to conceive which our natural powers would scarcely suffice."

This is our only hope, isn't it? If we were left on our own, our prayers could never attain a status of being worthy in God's sight, or perfect, as would befit the Lord. But God gives the Holy Spirit as our "teacher in prayer" to "tell us what is right" and to lead us to think and feel what God desires and seek his will.

Paul promises this: while "we do not know how to pray as we ought," the "very Spirit intercedes with sighs too deep for words" (Romans 8:26). Now we have the greatest hope as we pray! The Spirit takes our words, thoughts, and emotions and brings them into the divine presence!

PRAYER POINT: Ask God's Holy Spirit to take your words and bring them into God's presence.

True Faith Brings Forth Prayer

Romans 10:14–17

Prayer and faith are always related. Prayer is offered on the basis of true faith. True faith will always bring forth prayer.

Paul asked rhetorically, "How are they to call on one in whom they have not believed?" (Romans 10:14). If people do not believe in the God who has been revealed in Jesus Christ, they cannot—and will not—pray to him. Paul went on to argue for the necessity of Christian preaching—for this God who was revealed in Christ to be presented to and believed by the world (see vv. 14–17).

Faith and prayer are linked. According to Calvin, "the only true faith is that which brings forth prayer to God. It is impossible for a believer who has tasted the goodness of God ever to cease to aspire to that goodness in all his prayers." In prayer, our faith is exercised over and over again. In prayer, we remember the "goodness of God." This goodness of God forms the whole Christian story, which is the story of faith.

When we pray, it is important for us to recount the ways that the Christian story of redemption in Jesus Christ has been made real to us. We remember God's grace in creating us, his calling us to faith in Christ through the work of the Holy Spirit, his providence in leading and guiding us throughout our Christian lives, and the future of eternal life that he gives us. These form the fabric of our faith. In our prayers, let us always celebrate the "goodness of God"!

Reflection Question: In what ways would you speak of your own faith that leads you always to pray?

Persevere in Prayer

Romans 12:9–13

I T can be easy for us to become discouraged in our lives of prayer. As Christians, we seek to follow Paul's prescriptions for true Christians—to "rejoice in hope" and "be patient in suffering" (Romans 12:12). But we know that hope can flicker or falter, and patience during suffering is one of the most difficult things we have to deal with as disciples of Jesus Christ.

What do we do when we encounter these troubles . . . and many more?

Paul's next prescription to the Romans in verse 12 is to "persevere in prayer." This is one thing that we can do. We may not be able to manufacture hope or produce patience. But we can pray. We can pray and keep on praying.

Calvin wrote that "Paul not only stimulates us to prayer, but expressly calls for perseverance, because our warfare is unceasing and various assaults arise daily. Even the strongest are unable to bear these without frequent acquisition of new vigour. But diligence in prayer is the best remedy to prevent our being wearied."

Our experience with prayer teaches us that prayer is a practice in which we engage over the "long haul" of our lives. Praying and receiving a result is not usually instant. Throughout, and in the midst of, the tribulations and difficulties of life, we pray. We trust God to hear and answer us as we diligently pray throughout all seasons of our lives.

We need "new vigour," said Calvin, when life beats us down. Persevere in prayer!

REFLECTION QUESTION: As you look back on your prayer life through the years, what are ways you have found that prayer renews you, even when your hope is challenged or when you suffer?

G RANT, Almighty God, that since under the guidance of thy Son we have been united together in the body of thy Church, which has been so often scattered and torn asunder,—O grant, that we may continue in the unity of faith, and perseveringly fight against all the temptations of this world, and never deviate from the right course, whatever new troubles may daily arise: and though we are exposed to many deaths, let us not yet be seized with fear, such as may extinguish in our hearts every hope; but may we, on the contrary, learn to raise up our eyes and minds, and all our thoughts, to thy great power, by which thou quickenest the dead, and raisest from nothing things which are not, so that though we may be daily exposed to ruin, our souls may ever aspire to eternal salvation, until thou at length really showest thyself to be the fountain of life, when we shall enjoy that endless felicity, which has been obtained for us by the blood of thy only-begotten Son our Lord. Amen.

Reconciliation—by God's Gratuitous Favor

2 Corinthians 5:16–21

One of the most important things we should pray for in our lives is that we would live in a right relationship with God.

If we recognize that we are sinners—that we have lived life our way instead of God's way, have broken his commandments, and have fallen short of the love and trust that he wants us to have—then we are sinners who now realize that we need reconciliation with our creator.

Paul stresses God's great love, through which "in Christ God was reconciling the world to himself, not counting their trespasses against them" (2 Cor. 5:19). God chose to reconcile us in Jesus Christ—not because of who we are but because of who God is.

Calvin spoke about "God's gratuitous favor" in his comments on Jeremiah 36:7. He wrote, "For if any one only in words seeks to be reconciled to God, he will not succeed. Turning or conversion cannot be separated from prayer. But then were a sinner to repent a thousand times, he would still remain exposed to God's judgment; for reconciliation, by which we are absolved, does not depend on repentance, but on the gratuitous favour of God; for God does not receive us into favour because he sees that we are changed to a better mind, as though conversion were the cause of pardon; but he embraces us according to his gratuitous mercy."

Reconciliation with God does not depend on our work, our words, or our "repentance." God reconciles us not because of what we try to do. In Jesus Christ, his mercy—his pure grace—brings us the forgiveness and reconciliation that we need!

Reflection Question: Consider the difference between trying to reconcile ourselves with God and accepting God's gracious, loving mercy in Christ as our means of reconciliation.

We Don't Prescribe the Ways that God Answers

2 Corinthians 12:1–10

CALVIN notes that in many places Scripture says that God gives us whatever we ask for in faith. But Paul speaks of a "thorn" in his flesh (2 Corinthians 12:7), which he prayed three times for God to remove. It wasn't removed. Paul prayed in faith, but he did not obtain what he requested.

Calvin said that there are "two kinds of obtaining." One involves the things that we ask for with no qualifications, since they are promised to us with certainty in Scripture: God's kingdom, forgiveness, and so on. The other kind involves the things that we imagine are for our benefit—and about these we may be mistaken. Calvin said, "We ask for these things that are certainly promised with full confidence and without reserve, but it is not for us to prescribe the means, and if we do specify them, our prayer always has an unexpressed qualification included in it."

So we do not insist that God answer us in certain ways or through certain means. Often he uses ways that we do not expect. He answered Paul's prayer this way: "My grace is sufficient for you, for power is made perfect in weakness" (v. 9).

This makes prayer exciting! We believe that God hears and answers our prayers, but we never know when or how his answers will come. We don't get upset if the answers do not come in *our* way. We trust God to know what is best for us. We leave the means of God's answering our prayers up to him!

REFLECTION QUESTION: Think of those times when God answered your prayers in ways that you didn't expect. Were you alert to recognize these answers?

THE KEY TO THE KINGDOM OF HEAVEN

Ephesians 3:7–13

THERE is a great distance between us and God. This distance exists because we are humans and God is God. It also exists because of human sin. Sin breaks our relationship with God, separating us from the communion and trust God desires to have with those he has created.

In Jesus Christ, God has become a human being. Jesus died on the cross in order to forgive our sin and so that we can have "peace with God" (Rom. 5:1). Jesus opens access to God for us and enables us to pray in his name, giving us deep communion with God through faith.

Commenting on Ephesians 3:12, which says that in Christ Jesus our Lord "we have access to God in boldness and confidence through faith in him," Calvin wrote that God's children have "peace with God, and approach Him cheerfully and freely. We infer, likewise, from this passage that confidence is necessary in true invocation, and thus becomes the key that opens to us the gate of the kingdom of heaven."

Only Jesus Christ gives us the confidence to approach God in prayer. We can call on God, in intimate conversation, through Jesus Christ, who "intercedes for us" (Rom. 8:34). Our prayers do not need to be timid or fearful. We can approach God "cheerfully and freely," said Calvin, since we have "peace with God through our Lord Jesus Christ" (Rom. 5:1).

What a blessing! Jesus Christ opens the gate of the kingdom of heaven to us!

PRAYER POINT: Make a conscious effort to come to God freely and cheerfully while concentrating on Jesus Christ.

Continuing Our Prayers

Ephesians 6:18–20

M ANY times, our natural tendency is to do something once and then forget about it. But when we stop to think, we know that there are many things worth doing that take repetition and perseverance in order to be carried out. A result is achieved not after one try but after many tries.

So it is with prayer. The Ephesians are instructed to "always persevere in supplication for all the saints" (Eph. 6:18). Prayers are not to be offered only once and then forgotten. Prayer takes perseverance—a continuing practice of praying for others, for the world, and for ourselves, again and again.

Calvin captured this when he wrote about this verse: "We must press on cheerfully, lest we faint. With unabated ardour we must continue our prayers, though we do not immediately obtain what we desire."

We need this reminder to persevere in prayer. It would be easy for us to flit from one thing to another in our prayers. If we don't receive the answer that we want after a prayer or two, we move on to praying about something else. But our "ardour" and efforts must be unabated—we must continue to pray! We cannot expect God always to give us "instant results" in our prayers. Time and again we must petition God—not because he is stubborn or reluctant to answer us but because his will and purposes move according to his timing, not our own.

Continuing prayer should not be a burden for us; it should be a joy. We can approach God again . . . and again! This is our joy!

Reflection Question: Remember occasions when you have prayed many times about something. What was the result? Did you maintain cheerfulness as you continued to pray?

When We Are Cold in Prayer

Philippians 1:3–11

WHEN things are going well for us, we may get so busy and feel so self-sufficient that we neglect to pray. We want to feel blessed by God. But when those blessings turn us away from the source of all blessings, this is dangerous.

Paul was a person of prayer who urged all those in the churches that he visited or wrote to be zealous in prayer themselves—always. When times are good, pray. When times are bad, pray. As he wrote to the Philippians, he was "constantly praying with joy in every one of my prayers for all of you" (Phil. 1:4). He told them, "I thank my God every time I remember you" (v. 3)—and he remembered them most often by prayer.

We pray for others throughout all the seasons of their lives—when things are good for them and when they are bad for them. Their needs should rouse us to prayer. As Calvin wrote, "If, at any time, we are cold in prayer or more negligent than we ought to be, because we do not feel the pressure of immediate necessity, let us instantly reflect how many of our brethren are worn out by varied and heavy afflictions, are weighed down by deep anxiety, or are reduced to the worst distress. If we are not roused from our lethargy, we must have hearts of stone."

We are roused to prayer by the needs of others—or else we have "hearts of stone." When we are cold or neglectful in prayer, we must remember others!

REFLECTION QUESTION: What are ways that can help you to be more aware of others' needs and can motivate you to pray for them?

WHEN TEMPTED, PRAY!

Philippians 4:4–7

PAUL'S letter to the Philippians conveys the joyful vitality of Christian faith! In it, Paul provides a series of exhortations to the Philippian church. An important one is "Do not worry about anything, but in everything by prayer and supplication with thanksgiving let your requests be made known to God" (Philippians 4:6). No matter what issue we are presently facing, we can pray to God and let him know what our worries and anxieties are.

Our anxieties can be recognized as temptations. They turn us away from trusting in God and toward fretting about our current situations. Calvin noted that "we are not made of iron, so as to be unshaken by temptations. But our consolation, our relief, is to deposit, or (to speak more correctly) to unload into the bosom of God everything that harasses us. Confidence, it is true, brings tranquility to our minds, but only if we exercise ourselves in prayers. Whenever, therefore, we are assailed by any temptation, let us betake ourselves forthwith to prayer, as to a sacred refuge."

When we are faced with any kind of temptation, we should pray! God hears our prayers and helps us—and a time when we especially need God's help is when we are tempted. When cares and anxieties assail us and tempt us to turn away from relying on God, we should pray! We can give all things over to God, who answers our prayers and helps us—even when we are in the midst of experiencing temptations. So, when you are tempted, pray!

PRAYER POINT: Make it a point to recognize temptations and turn them over to God in prayer.

G RANT, Almighty God, that as thou hast deigned to
make thyself known to us by thy word, and as thou
elevatest us to thyself in a way suitable to the ignorance of
our minds,—O grant, that we may not continue fixed in our
stupidity, but that we may put off all superstitions, and also
renounce all the thoughts of our flesh, and seek thee in the
right way; and may we suffer ourselves to be so ruled by
thy word, that we may purely and from the heart call upon
thee, and so rely on thine infinite power, that we may not
fear to despise the whole world, and every adversity on the
earth, until, having finished our warfare, we shall at length
be gathered into that blessed rest, which thine only-begotten
Son has procured for us by his own blood.—Amen.

Assiduity and Alacrity

Colossians 4:1–4

O NE of the most important instructions for Christians to follow is simply to "devote yourselves to prayer" (Colossians 4:2). This word was vital to the Colossians, and it's vital to us today. A key practice for Christians is to pray . . . and to devote themselves to prayer continually.

Calvin used two terms we do not use much today in his comments on this verse. He wrote, "He [Paul] commends here two things in prayer; first, assiduity; secondly, alacrity, or earnest intentness. For when he says, 'Continue,' he exhorts them to perseverance; and he opposes 'watching' to coldness, and listlessness."

"Assiduity" means giving attention to something and persistently doing it. "Alacrity" means brisk and cheerful readiness.

These are good prescriptions, aren't they? We are to give attention to our prayers. We don't pray as a habit or treat prayer casually. If we are devoted to prayer, then it will be a primary focus for us. We will give strong attention to what we are doing as we pray persistently. Prayer is to be important for us—to be one of the primary things that we do as Christians.

Are we marked by a cheerful readiness to pray—by an eagerness and enthusiasm for praying? Do we come to prayer with a strong desire and enthusiastically anticipate being in conversation with God? Prayer is the "heartbeat" of our faith. It is our ongoing connection with our Lord, which we desire above all else and which gives our Christian lives vigor and vitality.

We persevere in prayer and participate in it eagerly. Let us practice assiduity and alacrity!

Reflection Question: What can help you to pray more persistently and eagerly?

GIVE THANKS

1 Thessalonians 5:12–24

W HAT is our attitude when we pray? Paul says that we should "pray without ceasing" (1 Thessalonians 5:17). This is a goal that we may never achieve. But when we do pray, what goes through our minds? What is our attitude toward God when we pray?

Paul goes on to say that we should "give thanks in all circumstances; for this is the will of God in Christ Jesus for you" (v. 18). No matter what our situation is, even if God has not immediately answered our prayers, we should be sure that all our prayers give thanksgiving to him—for who he is and what he has done. Calvin wrote that "many pray in such a way that they still murmur against God, and grumble if He does not immediately comply with their wishes. It is fitting, however, that our desires should be restrained so that we may be contented with what we are given, and always blend thanksgiving with our petitions. We may, it is true, entreat, and indeed groan and complain, but in such a way that the will of God becomes more acceptable to us than our own."

What should our attitudes be when we pray? No matter what goes through our minds or how we feel about how God is responding to us, we must always give thanks—must "blend thanksgiving with our petitions." This is God's will for us in Christ. We owe God all that we have—and all that we are. No wonder thanksgiving should be part of all our prayers!

PRAYER POINT: Spend time in prayer thanking God for the many specific things for which you are grateful.

Pray for Us

2 Thessalonians 3:1–5

WE often think that we are self-sufficient people. We manage all the dimensions of our lives. It's only when we run into things that are beyond our control that we recognize our need for assistance from others—or from God.

Sometimes we tell others, "I'll pray for you." We are willing to seek this source of divine help for them in whatever their circumstances may be. But are we equally willing to ask others to pray for us? This may require a higher level of courage and vulnerability from us than volunteering to pray for other people does. By asking for others to pray for us, we are admitting our need. We are seeking a source of help beyond our own power to handle the situations in which we find ourselves.

Paul was not bashful about asking others in the church to pray for him. He wrote, "Finally, brothers and sisters, pray for us" (2 Thessalonians 3:1). He asked the Thessalonians to pray that "the word of the Lord may spread rapidly and be glorified everywhere."

Calvin wrote, concerning this verse, that Paul "still has regard for the prayers of believers, by which the Lord wills to assist us. It is fitting that we too, following his example, should seek this aid and urge our brethren to pray for us."

In the church, we pray for others—and we ask others to pray for us. Mutuality of prayer is a mark of our fellowship with Christ and, in Christ, with one another—with the communion of saints. What a joy! What a blessing of being part of the church!

PRAYER POINT: Ask several people to pray for you, and include them in your own prayers daily.

Pray for Unknown Persons

1 Timothy 2:1–8

T HERE are many things that we can do for others. We spend
our Christian lives discovering what these may be. We
serve others through what we say, what we do, and how we look
out for their needs in various ways throughout their lives.

Calvin compared giving alms to people—giving to help
them monetarily—with praying for them. Giving alms means
being aware of someone's needs and helping to meet them. But,
Calvin said, there is a difference that sets praying apart from
this. For "we are free to help by prayer even utterly foreign and
unknown persons, however great the distance that separates
them from us." We can pray for people whom we don't know.
Calvin notes, in his comments on 1 Timothy 2:8, that in Christ
there are no differences between Gentiles and Jews "because
God is the common Father of them all." Earlier, concerning
1 Timothy 2:1—"I urge that supplications, prayers, interces-
sions, and thanksgivings be made for everyone"—Calvin wrote
that "whenever public prayers are offered, petitions and supplications should be made for all men, even those who at present
have no connexion with us."

Prayer for others—even those who are unknown to us—is an
important form of ministry. We do not know the specific needs
of others. But God does. In prayer, we can offer intercession for
others. We pray for people whom we do not know because they
are created by God, as we are. We are fellow humans. We can
pray that God meets their needs, whatever they may be. Always
pray for others!

Prayer Point: Think of the many people in places and
conditions that are unknown to you, and pray for them.

We May Safely Call on God

Hebrews 4:14–16

In the sixteenth century, Martin Luther asked the question "How do I find a gracious God?" God is holy, just, and righteous. As a human, Luther was sinful. His sin separated him from God. How could God be gracious to him? Luther came to believe that God is gracious toward sinners through Jesus Christ.

God loved the world and sent Jesus Christ to die for our sins. Jesus is the Great High Priest. He gave himself as the sacrifice that God accepts in order to forgive our sin. Through the gift of faith, we are accounted righteous in God's sight. God is gracious to us in Christ! So then, "let us therefore approach the throne of grace with boldness, so that we may receive mercy and find grace to help in time of need" (Hebrews 4:16).

Calvin wrote that "we may safely call on God, since we know that He is propitious [favorable] to us. This happens because of the mercy of Christ, as is stated in Eph. 3.12, because when Christ accepts us into His faith and discipleship, He covers with His goodness the majesty of God which could otherwise be fearful, so that nothing appears except grace and fatherly goodwill."

Now we may "safely call on God," since God is gracious to us! Our prayers come through Jesus Christ, our High Priest. We are reconciled to God in Christ. We can "approach the throne of grace with boldness" in prayer and find the mercy and grace that we need to help us.

Reflection Question: What are some ways that Jesus, as our Great High Priest, can make your prayer life deeper and richer?

Unapparent Answers to Prayers

Hebrews 5:1–10

Sometimes God's answers to our prayers are clear, and they come quickly. At other times . . . not so much!

But there are times as well when we can later see that God was at work in answering our prayers, even when it was not apparent to us earlier. God's will is at work in ways that we do not know or perceive. God is free to work when and how he wills—that's what God does!

For example, we see Jesus praying that the cup will pass from him (see Matt. 26:39). But, despite the fact that he "offered up prayers and supplications" (Heb. 5:7), Jesus went to his death. And yet from his death came our salvation. Through it, God was at work to accomplish the purposes of saving us.

Calvin said, "God often answers our prayers, even when it is least apparent. Although it is not for us to lay down any hard and fast rule for Him, nor is it in keeping for Him to have to grant our petitions in whatever frame of mind or form of words they are expressed, yet in every way in which He takes care for our salvation He shows that He has answered our prayers. So when we seem on the face of it to be repulsed, we get far more than if he had given us all we asked."

God helps us even when our prayers are—apparently—not being answered! Calvin said, "So when we seem on the face of it to be repulsed, we get far more than if He had given us all we asked." Thank God!

Reflection Question: What are some times when you thought that your prayers were not being answered but later saw how God was working in your life after all?

G RANT, Almighty God, that as almost the whole world breaks out into such excesses, that there is no moderation, no reason,—O grant, that we may learn not only to confine ourselves within those limits which thou dost approve and command, but also to delight and glory in the smallness of our portion, inasmuch as the wealth, and honours, and pleasures of the world so fascinate the hearts and minds of all, that they elevate themselves into heaven, and carry on war, as it were, avowedly with thee. Grant also to us, that in our limited portion we may be in such a way humbled under thy powerful hand, as never to doubt but that thou wilt be our deliverer even in our greatest miseries; and that ascribing to thee the power over life and death, we may feel fully assured, that whatever afflictions happen to us, proceed from thy just judgment, so that we may be led to repentance, and daily exercise ourselves in it, until we shall at length come to that blessed rest which is laid up for us in heaven, through Christ our Lord. Amen.

CHRIST'S INTERCESSION CONSECRATES OUR PRAYERS

Hebrews 13:7–16

Prayer is a theological act in which we express our deepest emotions to God through Jesus Christ. Jesus Christ is the "great high priest" (Heb. 4:14) who intercedes for us, as his people, before God (see Rom. 8:34).

Our prayers come to God through the intercession of Jesus Christ. He offered himself as the sacrifice for our sins (see Heb. 2:17). In him, all the former means of sacrifice no longer have power, since his sacrifice was "once for all when he offered himself" (Hebrews 7:27).

Now, as Christians, we offer ourselves in a "sacrifice of praise" (Heb. 13:15) when we pray and give thanks to God "without ceasing" (see 1 Thess. 5:17–18). This is the way we worship God as we celebrate his goodness by thanking him for all that he has done in Christ.

Calvin says that "by Christ's intercession are consecrated our prayers, which would otherwise have been unclean, so the apostle, enjoining us to offer a sacrifice of praise through Christ [Heb. 13:15], warns us that our mouths are not clean enough to sing the praises of God's name until Christ's priesthood intercedes for us."

This is our great assurance as we pray! Jesus consecrates our prayers by interceding for us before God. God sees us and hears our prayers through our Savior and High Priest, Jesus Christ. We are commanded and encouraged to pray by God, who receives all that we think and say in our prayers through the Son of God who has removed our sin "by the sacrifice of himself" (Hebrews 9:26). Let us pray and praise God!

REFLECTION QUESTION: What does Christ's role, as the High Priest who intercedes before God for us, mean to you?

LOOKING HOPEFULLY FOR GOD'S GRACE

James 1:5–7

J AMES teaches that if anyone is "lacking in wisdom, ask God, who gives to all generously and ungrudgingly, and it will be given you. But ask in faith, never doubting" (James 1:5–6). His prescription to us to "ask in faith" extends beyond this specific prayer and applies to all our praying.

We pray because we look to God. We look to him for help—of many kinds. The help that we most need from God is his grace. We pray for his grace and receive it as we pray in faith. Without faith, our praying avails nothing. As Calvin commented, "Our praying is a testimony that we look hopefully to God for the grace He has promised. A man who has no faith in the promises is praying in pretence."

Calvin continued, "Faith which relies on the promises of God assures us that we shall receive what we ask for: consequently, it goes with a confidence and a certainty of the love God has for us." Faith focuses on God's utter reliability as expressed in the promises that he makes. Throughout Scripture, God promises to answer our prayers (see Ps. 91:15; Isa. 65:24). His answers express his love for us. We can have "confidence and certainty" in God's love as the ground of our relationship with him and as the basis on which he answers our prayers.

God's response to our prayers comes entirely out of his grace. It is God's gracious desire to answer us when we pray. When we pray, we look for God's grace—with hope!

PRAYER POINT: Make it a point to pray for God's grace. Praise God for the grace that he gives—especially in the area of salvation.

GOD CALLS US TO PRAYER ALL THE TIME

James 5:13–14

THE book of James is a practical book that calls us to express our faith in all that we do. On the subject of prayer, it is realistic. It asks, "Are any among you suffering? They should pray" (James 5:13). The writer knew that suffering permeates human life. When suffering comes, the best thing we can do is to turn to God in prayer.

"They should pray" is good advice for all the seasons of our lives. Do we pray when we suffer? What about in times when we don't have a major issue like that? Do we pray then? Calvin said that "there is no time at which God does not call us to Himself. Sufferings should stimulate us to pray, prosperity should provide material for the praise of God. Here is a balance we must preserve, that the enjoyment which usually inclines us to be forgetful of God should stir us to declare His goodness, and the sorrows should give us a mind for prayer."

Do we strike this balance in our lives? Are we as quick to praise God and thank him for his goodness to us when we are enjoying life as when we are experiencing suffering and sorrow? When we are "at ease in Zion" (Amos 6:1) and things are good, do we rejoice in God? When suffering comes, do we seek first to pray for God's help?

In short, God calls us to pray all the time. Whatever we face in life—whether good or bad—we should come to God in prayer. Make prayer your first instinct, no matter what!

REFLECTION QUESTION: When are you more likely to pray—when things are good, or when things are bad? What can you do to establish a balance in your prayer life?

Touched by the Needs of Others

James 5:15–18

Over and over again, our wants drive us to pray. Meaningful prayer ought to reflect the realities of our life situations. Among these realities are the wants and desires that we have. We want, and so we pray.

But Calvin, recalling Paul's command to us to "pray without ceasing" (1 Thess. 5:17), wrote, "There is not a moment of our life at which our wants ought not to urge us to prayer. But there is another reason for praying without ceasing—that the necessities of our brethren ought to touch us. And when is it that some members of the Church are not in distress, and needing our assistance?" This captures the instruction that James gives us: "Pray for one another" (James 5:16).

We pray as an outpouring of our own wants, including our desire that the needs of others be met. In our prayers for one another, we ask for God's help for them. Their needs are many and great. James gives us the directive to pray for one another in the specific context of praying for the healing of others, but whatever their needs may be, we pray for others who are in need.

We should be touched by the needs of others, said Calvin, and thus we should pray for them. We should pray for those who are in our church community as well as for those who are unknown to us. There is never a time when those around us are not in distress and in need of our help. Praying for others seeks God's help for them—and God can help them through the help that we offer them ourselves. Pray for one another!

Prayer Point: Make a list of people you know who have needs. Use this list as you pray, and ask for God to help them—as well as for how you can help them yourself.

Praying in Faith and Hope

1 Peter 1:17–21

O UR prayers include our petitions to God. We ask God for what we desire—and what we trust is his will for us. Since God bids us to pray and to petition him, we believe that he hears and answers our prayers. We pray and keep on praying.

We invoke God, who has the will and power to answer our prayers. We know and believe that this is true by looking to the salvation that God gave us in Jesus Christ. In Christ, we see God's desire and power to save us. As Peter puts it, "Through him you have come to trust in God, who raised him from the dead and gave him glory, so that your faith and hope are set on God" (1 Peter 1:21). In Christ, we pray to God and receive from God.

Calvin said, "If we would pray fruitfully, we ought therefore to grasp with both hands this assurance of obtaining what we ask, which the Lord enjoins with his own voice, and all the saints teach by their example. For only that prayer is acceptable to God which is born, if I may so express it, out of such presumption of faith, and is grounded in unshaken assurance of hope."

Faith and hope are indivisibly bound together in prayer. We pray in faith, believing that God hears and answers. We hope for the things that we pray for, expressing faith and trust that God in his loving providence will answer our prayers. Hope gives us assurance, and faith expresses our trust, as we pray. Pray in faith and hope!

REFLECTION QUESTION: When you pray, do you bring to mind that you are praying in faith and in hope? In what ways does this recognition encourage and strengthen your prayers?

Pray According to God's Will

1 John 5:14–17

W E pray for many things. But there is one thing we must keep in mind: our prayers are always to be aimed at doing God's will. We have great confidence when we pray. God hears and answers our prayers. But our requests are to be in submission to what God wants for us. We see this in 1 John 5:14: "And this is the boldness we have in him, that if we ask anything according to his will, he hears us."

It is not that we lay before God whatever comes into our minds. God's "rule" for our prayer is that we subject our own wishes to his plan and purposes. We ourselves do not know what is best for us. God does. So our prayers should seek to be in accordance with his will. Calvin commented, "God does not allow his gentle dealing to be thus mocked but, claiming his own right, he subjects our wishes to his power and bridles them. For this reason, we must hold fast to John's statement: 'This is the confidence we have in him, that if we ask anything according to his will, he hears us' [1 John 5:14]." Our petitions when we pray should be in accordance with God's will for us.

How do we know God's will? God has given us his Word—the Scriptures. He has given us his Spirit to reveal his will. We should ask God to direct our minds, hearts, and wills to have the deep desire to always seek his will when we pray.

Reflection Question: What are ways that we can keep God's will foremost in our prayers?

Gifts Given by the Spirit

Jude 17–23

THERE are times when we may grow lazy and cold in our prayers. These times may creep up on us and keep us from realizing that our prayer lives are lessened—or even dormant.

When these times come, we need to realize the vital role that the Holy Spirit plays in our prayers. The Spirit stirs us to pray and deepens our prayers before the throne of God (see Rom. 8:26). So when we encounter times of difficulty in our prayers, we should pray for the Spirit to energize us and prompt prayer within us.

The book of Jude says, "Pray in the Holy Spirit" (v. 20). In his comments on this verse, Calvin mentioned that "none can succeed in praying as he ought without the prompting of the Spirit of God" and that we can "lose heart" and do not even dare to call God "Father" unless the Spirit "puts the word into us." It is "from the Spirit, we receive the gift of real concern, ardour, forcefulness, eagerness, confidence that we shall receive—all these, and finally those groanings which cannot be uttered, as Paul writes (Rom. 8.26). Jude does well indeed to say that no-one can pray as he ought to pray, unless the Spirit direct him."

When problems arise in our prayers, we can ask God's Spirit to work—to give us his gifts of interest, passion, strength, readiness, and sureness—so that we can pray. We cannot pray as we "ought," or even pray at all, unless the Spirit directs us. Pray for the Spirit to direct your prayer!

PRAYER POINT: Make special efforts to ask the Spirit of God to lead you to pray and to direct your prayers.

G RANT, Almighty God, that as thou hast made us a royal priesthood in thy Son, that we may daily offer to thee spiritual sacrifices, and be devoted to thee, both in body and soul,—O grant, that we, being endued with thy power, may boldly fight against Satan, and never doubt but that thou wilt finally give us the victory, though we may have to undergo many troubles and difficulties: and may not the contempt of the world frighten or dishearten us, but may we patiently bear all our reproaches, until thou at length stretchest forth thine hand to raise us up to that glory, the perfection of which now appears in our head, and shall at last be clearly seen in all the members, in the whole body, even when he shall come to gather us into that celestial kingdom, which he has purchased for us by his own blood.—Amen.

Notes

U NLESS otherwise indicated, each note gives the source of all quotations by Calvin on the corresponding page. Notes containing more than one citation describe, for each citation, the location on the corresponding page of any quotations that come from its source.

18   Prayer following commentary on Jeremiah 1:12.

19   Commentary on Genesis 32:22.

20   Commentary on Numbers 14:17.

21   Quotation in first paragraph: James Montgomery, "Prayer Is the Soul's Sincere Desire," 1818; quotation in second paragraph: *Institutes* 3.20.33.

22   Quotations in second paragraph: *Institutes* 3.20.4; quotation in third paragraph: *Institutes* 3.20.5.

23   Commentary on Psalm 10:13.

24   *Institutes* 3.20.2.

25   Prayer following commentary on Jeremiah 2:19.

26   Commentary on Psalm 17:1.

27   Commentary on Psalm 18:6.

28   *Institutes* 3.20.16.

29   *Institutes* 3.20.51.

30   *Institutes* 3.20.5.

31   Second quotation in second paragraph and all quotations in third and fourth paragraphs: Commentary on Psalm 25:22; quotation in fifth paragraph: Joseph M. Scriven, "What a Friend We Have in Jesus," 1855.

32 Prayer following commentary on Lamentations 3:39.

33 *Institutes* 3.20.51.

34 Commentary on Psalm 30:8.

35 Commentary on Psalm 32:6.

36 Commentary on Psalm 50:15.

37 *Institutes* 3.20.16.

38 Commentary on Psalm 55:22.

39 Prayer at commentary on Lamentations 5:13.

40 *Institutes* 3.20.52.

41 Commentary on Psalm 56:9.

42 *Institutes* 3.20.12.

43 Commentary on Psalm 86:3.

44 *Institutes* 3.20.50.

45 Commentary on Psalm 91:15.

46 Prayer following commentary on Ezekiel 20:44.

47 Commentary on Psalm 102:2.

48 Commentary on Psalm 102:17.

49 *Institutes* 3.20.12.

50 Commentary on Psalm 119:58.

51 *Institutes* 3.20.4.

52 Commentary on Psalm 143:2.

53 Prayer following commentary on Daniel 1:3.

54 Commentary on Psalm 145:19.

55 *Institutes* 3.20.15.

56 Commentary on Isaiah 63:16.

57 Commentary on Isaiah 65:24.

58 Commentary on Jeremiah 29:12.

59 *Institutes* 3.20.14.

60 Prayer following commentary on Daniel 2:2.

61 Commentary on Jeremiah 36:7.

62 Commentary on Lamentations 3:21.

63 Commentary on Daniel 6:10.

64 Commentary on Daniel 9:2.

65 *Institutes* 3.20.8.

66 Commentary on Daniel 10:12.

67 Prayer following commentary on Hosea 13:13.

68   Commentary on Joel 2:32.

69   Commentary on Micah 3:4.

70   Commentary on Habakkuk 1:3.

71   Commentary on Matthew 6:5.

72   Commentary on Matthew 6:8.

73   Commentary on Matthew 6:9.

74   Prayer at commentary on Joel 2:28.

75   Commentary on Matthew 6:13.

76   Commentary on Matthew 7:9.

77   Commentary on Matthew 9:29.

78   Commentary on Matthew 21:9.

79   *Institutes* 3.20.2.

80   Commentary on Matthew 26:39.

81   Prayer following commentary on Amos 2:13.

82   Commentary on Mark 9:22.

83   Commentary on Matthew 21:21.

84   *Institutes* 3.20.44.

85   Commentary on Luke 11:5.

86   First quotation in third paragraph: *Institutes* 3.20.6; all other quotations in third paragraph: Commentary on John 11:3.

87   Commentary on John 15:7.

88   Prayer following commentary on Obadiah 21.

89   Commentary on Acts 1:14.

90   Commentary on Romans 1:9.

91   Commentary on Romans 8:26.

92   *Institutes* 3.20.5.

93   Commentary on Romans 10:14.

94   Commentary on Romans 12:12.

95   Prayer following commentary on Micah 4:10.

96   Commentary on Jeremiah 36:7.

97   Commentary on 2 Corinthians 12:8.

98   Commentary on Ephesians 3:12.

99   Commentary on Ephesians 6:18.

100 Commentary on Ephesians 6:18.

101 Commentary on Philippians 4:6.

102 Prayer following commentary on Habakkuk 3:1.

103 Commentary on Colossians 4:2.

104 Commentary on 1 Thessalonians 5:17.

105 Commentary on 2 Thessalonians 3:1.

106 First quotation in second paragraph: *Institutes* 3.20.39; second quotation in second paragraph: Commentary on 1 Timothy 2:8; fourth quotation in second paragraph: Commentary on 1 Timothy 2:1.

107 Commentary on Hebrews 4:16.

108 Commentary on Hebrews 5:7.

109 Prayer following commentary on Zephaniah 1:12.

110 *Institutes* 3.20.28.

111 Commentary on James 1:6.

112 Commentary on James 5:13.

113 Commentary on Ephesians 6:18.

114 *Institutes* 3.20.12.

115 *Institutes* 3.20.5.

116 Commentary on Jude 20.

117 Prayer following commentary on Zechariah 3:4.

Works Cited

Calvin's Old Testament Commentaries

Calvin, John. *Commentaries on the First Book of Moses Called Genesis*. Translated by John King. Vol 2. Edinburgh, 1850.

———. *Commentaries on the Four Last Books of Moses, Arranged in the Form of a Harmony*. Translated by Charles William Bingham. Vol 4. Edinburgh, 1855.

———. *Commentary on the Book of Psalms*. Translated by James Anderson. 5 vols. Edinburgh, 1845–49.

———. *Commentary on the Book of the Prophet Isaiah*. Translated by William Pringle. Vol 4. Edinburgh, 1853.

———. *Commentaries on the Book of the Prophet Jeremiah and the Lamentations*. Translated and edited by John Owen. Vol 1. Edinburgh, 1850.

———. *Commentaries on the Book of the Prophet Jeremiah and the Lamentations*. Translated and edited by John Owen. Vol 3. Edinburgh, 1852.

———. *Commentaries on the Book of the Prophet Jeremiah and the Lamentations*. Translated and edited by John Owen. Vol 4. Edinburgh, 1854.

———. *Commentaries on the Book of the Prophet Jeremiah and the Lamentations*. Translated and edited by John Owen. Vol 5. Edinburgh, 1855.

———. *Commentaries on the First Twenty Chapters of the Book of the Prophet Ezekiel*. Translated by Thomas Myers. Vol. 2. Edinburgh, 1850.

———. *Commentaries on the Book of the Prophet Daniel.* Translated by Thomas Myers. 2 vols. Edinburgh, 1852–53.

———. *Commentaries on the Twelve Minor Prophets.* Translated by John Owen. 5 vols. Edinburgh, 1846–49.

Calvin's New Testament Commentaries

Calvin, John. *A Harmony of the Gospels: Matthew, Mark and Luke.* Vol. 1. Translated by A. W. Morrison. Calvin's New Testament Commentaries 1. Reprint, Grand Rapids: William B. Eerdmans, 1980.

———. *A Harmony of the Gospels: Matthew, Mark and Luke.* Vol. 2. Translated by T. H. L. Parker. Calvin's New Testament Commentaries 2. Reprint, Grand Rapids: William B. Eerdmans, 1979.

———. *A Harmony of the Gospels: Matthew, Mark and Luke.* Vol. 3, *And the Epistles of James and Jude.* Translated by A.W. Morrison. Calvin's New Testament Commentaries 3. Reprint, Grand Rapids: William B. Eerdmans, 1980.

———. *The Gospel According to St. John 11–21 and The First Epistle of John.* Translated by T. H. L. Parker. Calvin's New Testament Commentaries 5. Reprint, Grand Rapids: Wm. B. Eerdmans, 1979.

———. *The Acts of the Apostles 1–13.* Translated by John W. Fraser and W. J. G. McDonald. Calvin's New Testament Commentaries 6. Reprint, Grand Rapids: William B. Eerdmans, 1979.

———. *The Epistles of Paul The Apostle to the Romans and to the Thessalonians.* Translated by Ross Mackenzie. Calvin's New Testament Commentaries 8. Grand Rapids: William B. Eerdmans, 1961.

———. *The Second Epistle of Paul The Apostle to the Corinthians and the Epistles to Timothy, Titus and Philemon.* Translated by T. A. Smail. Calvin's New Testament Commentaries 10. Reprint, Grand Rapids: William B. Eerdmans, 1979.

———. *The Epistles of Paul The Apostle to the Galatians, Ephesians, Philippians and Colossians.* Translated by T. H. L. Parker. Calvin's New Testament Commentaries 11. Reprint, Grand Rapids: William B. Eerdmans, 1980.

———. *The Epistle of Paul The Apostle to the Hebrews and The First and Second Epistles of St. Peter.* Translated by William B. Johnston.

Calvin's New Testament Commentaries 12. Grand Rapids: William B. Eerdmans, 1963.

Other

Calvin: Institutes of the Christian Religion. Edited by John T. McNeill. Translated by Ford Lewis Battles. 2 vols. The Library of Christian Classics. Philadelphia: The Westminster Press, 1960.

SELECTED RESOURCES FOR FURTHER REFLECTION

Battles, Ford Lewis, trans. and ed. *The Piety of John Calvin: A Collection of His Spiritual Prose, Poems, and Hymns.* 1978. Reprint, Phillipsburg, NJ: P&R Publishing, 2009.

Beeke, Joel R. "Calvin on Piety." In *The Cambridge Companion to John Calvin,* edited by Donald K. McKim, 125–52. New York: Cambridge University Press, 2004.

Bloesch, Donald G. *The Struggle of Prayer.* New York: Harper & Row, 1980.

Calvin, John. *On Prayer: Conversation with God.* Louisville: Westminster John Knox Press, 2006.

Leith, John H. *John Calvin's Doctrine of the Christian Life.* Louisville: Westminster John Knox Press, 1989.

McKee, Elsie Anne, ed. *John Calvin: Writings on Pastoral Piety.* The Classics of Western Spirituality. Mahwah, NJ: Paulist Press, 2001.

McKee, Elsie Anne. "John Calvin's Teaching on the Lord's Prayer." In *The Lord's Prayer: Perspectives for Reclaiming Christian Prayer,* edited by Daniel L. Migliore, 88–106. Grand Rapids: Wm. B. Eerdmans, 1993.

Wallace, Ronald S. *Calvin's Doctrine of the Christian Life.* Reprint, Eugene, OR: Wipf & Stock, 1997.

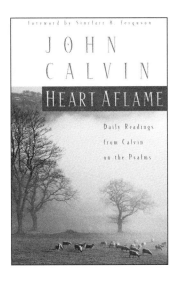

John Calvin described the Psalms as "an anatomy of all the parts of the soul."

These select readings from his *Commentary on the Psalms* provide us with a year's worth of sure-footed daily meditations. Calvin wrote as one whose own experience is mirrored in the Psalms. Here we witness his remarkable knack for seeing the real issues—particularly how Christ is the focus of all Scripture.

"An outstanding physician and surgeon of the spirit . . . [Calvin] had learned the meaning of the command to love God 'with all your mind.' . . . Reading [these meditations] on a daily basis can hardly fail to bring you spiritual health and strength."
—**Sinclair B. Ferguson**

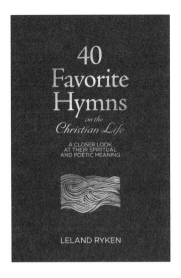

Did you enjoy this book?
Consider writing a review online.
The author appreciates your feedback!

Or write to P&R at editorial@prpbooks.com
with your comments. We'd love to hear from you.